Getting Started in

Hedge
Funds

The Getting Started In Series

Getting Started in
Hedge
Funds

Daniel A. Strachman

John Wiley & Sons, Inc.
New York • Chichester • Weinheim • Brisbane • Singapore • Toronto

Copyright © 2000 by Daniel A. Strachman. All rights reserved.

Published by John Wiley & Sons, Inc.

Published simultaneously in Canada.

This publication is designed to provide accurate and authoritative information in regard to the subject matter covered. It is sold with the understanding that the publisher is not engaged in rendering professional services. If professional advice or other expert assistance is required, the services of a competent professional person should be sought.

Library of Congress Cataloging-in-Publication Data:

Strachman, Daniel A., 1971–
      Getting started in hedge funds / Daniel A. Strachman.
        p.   cm. — (Getting started in series)
      Includes bibliographical references and index.
      ISBN 0-471-31696-2 (pbk. : alk. paper)
      1. Hedge funds.   I. Title.   II. Getting started in.
    HG4530.S837   2000
    332.64'5—dc21
                                                99-047273

Printed in the United States of America.

10 9 8 7 6 5 4 3 2 1

To
My Parents

Acknowledgments

The idea for this book has been in my head for more than five years. It really jelled, however, when Ivy Schmerken gave me the opportunity to write stories for a magazine she was launching called *Financial Trader*. Through a little bit of salesmanship and a lot of luck, I somehow persuaded Ivy to allow me to write a column about traders—more specifically, hedge fund managers. When she passed the editor's torch to Lee Montgomery, he continued to provide me with the venue to write about what I wanted, as did the third and final editor of the magazine, Laure Edwards. Unfortunately, in March of 1998, the magazine stopped publication. To Ivy, Lee, and Laure, I say thank you.

I had just finished reading Jack Schwager's *Market Wizards* and *The New Market Wizards* when Ivy offered me the opportunity to write the columns. My thought was that if he could write two books about traders, I could at least put together my columns into a volume about hedge fund managers. This idea gave me the drive to write the columns. Every story I had written for newspapers and magazines ended with the last period on the last page. Now, however, I had a goal. This was a totally new concept for me as a journalist. After about three years of writing the columns, I realized that I had enough to put together an outline for a book. In October 1997, I decided that the column would be no more and I would concentrate on getting a book published.

This was a formidable task, but in the fall of 1997 I was talking to Ira Kawaller, whom I knew from working on the Street. He suggested I speak with Schwager. I was reluctant, but called and Schwager introduced me to Pamela van Giessen, an editor at John Wiley & Sons. She reviewed my proposal, told me it was no good, and asked for another. The result is this book. To Ira, Jack, and Pamela, thank you very much.

A number of people were very helpful in making this book a reality.

Three are Peter Testaverde, Sam Graff, and Sarah Theodore. Peter is in a league of his own when it comes to understanding the hedge fund business and knowing people in the industry. Although I am sure Peter did not always like getting calls and buying me lunch, I am entirely grateful for all of his help. Sam is the only true newspaperman I have ever known. He is a wordsmith unlike anyone I have ever encountered and I appreciate his help and guidance with the text of this book. Sarah is a testament to librarians and researchers around the world. Her understanding of information sources is unbelievable and her ability to find things is truly amazing. I want to thank her for finding stories and material that I had no idea existed as well as for finding ones that I thought she would never be able to locate.

If I don't thank Howard Lasher, Steve Hamrick, and Jeff Zack, I will probably never be able to show my head either in the old place, in the new place, or on Trinity Place ever again. Howard is truly one of a kind when it comes to those who work on Wall Street. I offer my sincere gratitude for all the help he provided to me for this book. Steve, thanks for giving me a push when I needed it, and Jeff, thanks for giving your honest opinion about my work. It is an honor to call each of you a friend.

I also want to thank Valerie Garfield; without her help and continued belief in me, this book would not have been possible.

Of course, I need to thank all of the Midas traders and people in the industry who agreed to be interviewed. Had they not been so forthcoming, there would be no book. I hope that I captured their thoughts and comments the way they intended.

My sincere thanks also to Annette, Stanley, David, Ruth, Amy, and Alison for their support and guidance throughout this project.

Finally, I wish to thank all of those people at John Wiley & Sons who provided me with the opportunity to write this book and for helping to make me look good in print. I greatly appreciate their faith in this unknown writer and hope that this book is everything they intended it to be when they gave me the go-ahead to write it.

DANIEL A. STRACHMAN

Contents

Chapter 4

Hedge Fund Investing   159

Conclusion   185

Appendix

Hedge Fund Strategies   189

Glossary   193

Endnotes   197

Index   201

— Getting Started in —
Hedge Funds

The Midas Traders

I n the past five years, hedge funds have gone from relative obscurity to being a topic of cocktail party chatter and reports on the evening news.

Hedge funds and those who manage and invest in them have become the most talked about investment outside of Internet initial public offerings (IPOs). The rise from obscurity began with the astronomical returns that many hedge funds posted during the euphoria that has swept the investment world in recent years. Now, the interest has been sparked by the opposite: spectacular losses racked up in the past year and a half by many of the hedge fund world's most famous and sought-after managers. In early 1998, the issues for investors were "How do I invest?" and "How much can I expect?" In late 1998 and throughout most of 1999, the issue became "How do I get my money out and is there any left?" It seemed that the period from late 1998 through most of 1999 was the year and a half of the hedge fund. Once again, the greed that was deemed good in the 1980s was back in favor among investors.

When some of the investment world's biggest and brightest stars began posting huge losses, shock waves rippled from Wall Street to Main Street. People did not want to believe that these Midas traders could make such drastic mistakes. Since the initial stories broke, the markets have turned for the better. As can be expected, some funds were able to stop the hemorrhaging, having been left with significantly less money under management. Others have seen their funds grow by leaps and bounds. In the midst of the carnage many pundits believed that the hedge fund business was finished. The truth is exactly the opposite. Hedge funds are here to stay. Sure, some may be wiped out or close their doors voluntarily, but there will always be someone else willing to open another hedge fund.

Not only are hedge funds thriving, the *prime brokers*, lawyers, and accountants who service them are, too. The reason? Wall Street is about making money—and running a hedge fund provides one of the greatest ways to do it.

prime broker   service offered by major brokerage firms providing clearance, settlement, and custody functions for hedge funds.

This book is intended to provide an overview of the hedge fund industry. It covers many of the most important subjects surrounding running and investing in these investment vehicles. Certainly there is no one way to invest in hedge funds, as there are so many different funds with just as many different investment strategies and philosophies. A key goal of this book is to provide an objective view of the industry, one that gives you an understanding of the complex world of hedge funds that has dramatically changed since the concept was created in the late 1940s.

The growing importance and impact of hedge funds make it a subject that all investors should seek to understand. That's especially true because there are so many misconceptions about the industry.

Today, many people outside Wall Street believe that Long-Term Capital Management LP and George Soros are representative of the entire hedge fund industry. This is just not the case. Although it is difficult to put an exact number on it, at last count there were over 3,000 hedge funds with roughly $500 billion under management. While the Soros organization is considered by most to be the biggest hedge fund manager and Long-Term Capital is probably the most notorious hedge fund, they are a far cry from representing the entire industry. The industry stretches all over the world and ranges from men and women who manage titanic sums of money to those who manage a relative pittance.

The common perception is quite different from reality. The perception of the hedge fund world is that of gunslingers and traders who manage billions of dollars by the seat of their pants. The reality is that most hedge funds have far less than $100 million under management and, in most cases, every single trade that is executed is a calculated move. But no matter how often or how much the managers talk to the press, they can't seem to shed the stigma of being a gunslinger. A careful look, however, will show there is probably more risk to investing in an ordinary mutual fund than in most hedge funds. This is because hedge fund managers put their money where their mouths are. All hedge funds have some—if not all—of their managers' wealth invested in them. The losses or gains directly affect the size of their own bank accounts along with those of their investors.

People who think that hedge funds are run by ruthless men and women looking to make a buck at any cost do not understand the basic concept of hedge fund management. While a few managers may operate in this fashion, most do not. Most are interested in two things: preserving capital and making money for their partners. If you ask managers what is the most important aspect of their business, they will tell you: the preservation of capital. It takes money to make money. If you lose capital, you limit your resources to invest further and you soon will be out of business. By limiting risk and not betting the ranch on a single investment, they will live to invest another day. For hedge fund managers, slow and steady wins the race. The men and women who run hedge funds are some of the most dedicated money managers

3

in the world. This shows in their ability to continually outperform the market.

There is a big difference between hedge funds and mutual funds. The first is the size of the industry. The largest hedge fund complex has under $20 billion in assets under management while the largest mutual fund has over $100 billion in assets under management. All mutual funds are highly regulated by the Securities and Exchange Commission (SEC) and are open to any and all investors, assuming they can meet the minimum investment requirements. Hedge funds are not open to the general public, only to accredited investors and institutions. Accredited investors as defined by the Securities and Exchange Commission are individuals who have a net worth of a million dollars or who have had net income of $200,000 in the past two years and have reasonable expectations of continued income at that level. Hedge funds are not even allowed to advertise.

derivatives securities that take their values from another security.

The SEC does not allow mutual fund managers to use *derivatives* or to sell securities short to enhance performance. Hedge funds can use any legal means necessary to produce results. Most mutual fund managers are paid on the basis of the amount of assets they attract, while hedge fund managers are paid for performance. Unlike mutual fund investing, hedge fund investing is about calculating how to perform in good and bad markets through the use of investment strategies that consist of *long positions* and *short positions*. While mutual fund managers are limited to taking long positions in stocks and bonds, Midas traders are able to use a much more extensive array of investment strategies such as the use of shorting and derivatives. It is all about capital preservation and healthy returns. While the differences do not end there, I believe those are the most important.

long position a transaction to purchase shares of a stock resulting in a net positive position.

In the large hedge fund complexes, such as the George Soros and Julian Robertson organizations, accountability for the funds rests with multiple managers, analysts, and traders. In smaller organizations, the funds are accountable to a single individual. Most hedge fund organizations usually consist of a small staff working with the manager. While the size and scope of the organizations vary, all hedge funds seek to provide investors with a valuable service: capital preservation mixed with healthy returns. The common theme among all hedge fund managers is to use investment strategies that create a diversified portfolio that over time will outperform the market regardless of market conditions.

The purpose of this book is to provide an introduction that explores these types of operations. I purposely did not examine managers and funds that are covered in the popular press. Instead I spent time getting to know managers who are known on Wall Street but not outside it. They manage portfolios ranging in size from $2 million to over $2 billion. In some cases they operate by themselves out of a small office with one assistant. Others have multiple offices around the globe with staffs of a hundred or more.

short position a transaction to sell shares of stock that the investor does not own.

The idea of the book is to provide you with a clearer view at how these people operate in the various markets that they trade. Because each employs different trading methodologies and investment philosophies, this book provides you with a unique look at the business of managing money. It will, I hope, give you the insight you need to find

5

alternative means to achieve your investment goals. While all the managers are different, they all have two things in common: They use some piece of the same business model and each is an entrepreneur.

While profiles of managers make up a significant portion of this book, other pages describe the history of the industry and how it has evolved. George Soros, Michael Steinhardt, and Julian Robertson, unlike what many have been led to believe, did not create the hedge fund. While they may have advanced the concept, the idea and the term were created by journalist Alfred Winslow Jones, a visionary who took his knowledge of sociology and his reporting skills and came up with the idea in the late 1940s while researching an article for *Fortune* magazine.

Jones's basic concept is simple: By combining the use of long and short positions coupled with the use of *leverage*, a manager should be able to outperform the market in good times and to limit losses in bad times. Today most hedge funds employ the same concept. Like everything else, however, each manager uses his or her own unique style and therefore some may use more leverage than others, and some may not go short at all. All are out to beat the indexes while limiting losses. The right way to look at hedge fund performance is by absolute returns, regardless of market conditions.

leverage   means of enhancing return or value without increasing investment. Buying securities on margin is an example of leverage.

Hedge funds continue to thrive because this concept works.

Evidence lies in the number of people and firms that have grown to support hedge funds. Many of these supporting cast members believe that providing goods and services to the industry will be just as profitable as investing in or operating a hedge fund. These people range from consultants and brokers to lawyers and accountants. It is very easy to find a firm that will not only recommend a manager to potential investors but also help a manager find office space and set up phone lines. People from all walks of Wall Street have gotten into the hedge fund business, making it relatively easy not only to open a hedge fund but to learn about and invest in one as well.

To understand how hedge funds operate, you need to understand the styles and strategies their managers use. While most conventional money managers own securities in hopes of price appreciation, many hedge fund managers employ alternative strategies that do not rely on the market's going up: short selling, risk *arbitrage*, and the trading of derivatives. Most hedge funds employ strategies that allow them to hedge against risk to ensure that no matter which way the market moves, they are protected against loss.

arbitrage   a financial transaction involving simultaneous purchase in one market and sale in a different market.

There are many benefits to investing hedge funds. First, I believe that the best and brightest minds in money management have migrated from mutual funds and brokerages to the private world of hedge funds. Paying managers for performance ensures that the investor is going to get the fairest shake to begin with. Add the fact that managers have their own money in the fund and that should be enough for investors to know that their money is in good hands.

As an investor, however, you need to understand what you are getting into and be willing to do research to learn about the manager and the various strategies employed. One of the biggest mistakes people make with any kind of investing is not taking the time to do research. A smart investor is a well-researched investor. If a manager is unwilling to spend time discussing strategy, skills, and background, then investors probably should look elsewhere.

Another mistake is chasing so-called hot money—which is money that flows to the best-performing manager for a quarter or two. The right thing to do is to find managers who perform consistently over time. As an investor you should expect up months and quarters and down months and quarters and, more important, information regarding both periods. It is important to understand where the manager's performance is or is not coming from.

One of the basic tenets of sound investing is portfolio diversification. You should expect managers to explain how they employ it in their portfolios. One of the greatest lessons of the near self-destruction of Long-Term Capital is the need for investors to understand how and where their money is being invested. The idea that a manager wants an investor to have blind faith is ridiculous. Managers should be held accountable and investors should demand to know what is being done with their money.

Despite lapses by some managers and all the media attention, writing this book has made it even more obvious to me that hedge funds are good for investors and managers alike. I believe that by the time you are done reading this book you will believe this as well.

Chapter

Hedge Fund Basics

For most of the 1990s, the only time the press mentioned hedge funds was when one blew up or some sort of crisis hit one of the world's many markets. All that changed in the late summer of 1998. The currency crisis in Asia spread to Russia, then crept into Europe, and finally hit the shores of the United States in mid-July and early August. Many who follow the markets assumed that things were bad and were going to stay that way for a very long time. And of course the first people who were looked at when the volatility hit was the hedge fund community. Although no one knew for sure what was going on and who and how much was lost, one thing was clear: Many of the most famous hedge funds were in trouble.

After weeks of speculation and rumors, the market finally heard the truth: The world's greatest investor and his colleagues had made a mistake. At a little before 4 P.M. eastern standard time (EST) on Wednesday, August 26, Stanley Druckenmiller made the announcement on CNBC in a matter-of-fact way: The Soros organization, in particular its flagship hedge fund, the Quantum Fund, had lost more than $2 billion in recent weeks in the wake of the currency crisis in Russia. The fund had invested heavily in the Russian markets and the trades had gone against them. When the ruble collapsed, the liquidity dried up and there was nothing left to do but hold on to a bunch of worthless slips of paper. During the interview, Druckenmiller did mention that although the fund had sustained significant losses in its Russian investments, overall its total return was still positive for the year, with gains upwards of 19 percent. However, in the months that followed, the Soros organization announced significant changes to the operation including closing one fund that lost over 30 percent.

When asked by the CNBC reporter where the losses came from, Druckenmiller was not specific. It appeared that it was not one trade but a series of trades that had gone against them. The next day, *The New York Times* reported that the fund had also posted losses in dollar bond trades.

When Druckenmiller made the announcement, the Russian equity markets had been down over 80 percent and the government had frozen currency trading as well as stopped paying interest on its debts. The Asian flu had spread, and Russia and many of the other former Soviet republics looked to be in trouble. The difference was that in Russia and the surrounding countries, things looked quite a bit worse than in east Asia.

Although there had been rumors of hedge fund misfortunes and mistakes in these regions, no one knew the true size and scope of the losses. Druckenmiller's announcement was the tip of a very big iceberg and the beginning of a trend in the hedge fund industry, one that was a first: to be open and honest about losses. Hedge fund managers en masse seemed to be stepping up to the plate and admitting publicly that they had made mistakes and had sustained significant losses.

The day after the Soros organization spoke up, a number of other hedge fund managers issued similar statements. Druckenmiller's interview turned out to be the first of several such admissions of losses by famed fund managers. And the losses were staggering.

One fund lost over 85 percent of its assets, going from over $300 million to around $25 million under management. Another said it had lost over $200 million. Others lost between 10 and 20 percent of their assets. They all had come out publicly to lick their wounds, a sort of Wall Street mea culpa.

When the carnage first hit, it seemed that everyone except Julian Robertson, the mastermind behind Tiger Management, the second-largest hedge fund complex in the world, was the only "name" fund manager not to post losses. Yet even that proved not to be true.

In a statement on September 16, 1998, Robertson said that his funds had lost $2.1 billion or 10 percent of the $20-odd billion he had under management. The losses seemed to come in the early part of September and stemmed from a long-profitable bet on the yen's continuing to fall against the dollar. Because the yen instead appreciated, a number of Robertson's trades declined in value.[1] The funds also saw losses on trades executed in Hong Kong when government authorities intervened in the stock and futures markets to ward off foreign speculators.

Still, like Soros, Tiger was up significantly for the first eight months of 1998. These numbers echoed the funds' performance in recent years with returns in 1996 of over 38 percent and in 1997 of 56 percent. In a letter to investors explaining the losses, Robertson cautioned that the volatility of various markets would make it difficult to continue to post positive returns month after month.

"Sometimes we are going to have a very bad month," he wrote. "We are going to lose money in Russia and in our U.S. longs, and the diversification elsewhere is not going to make up for that, at least not right away. You should be prepared for this."

One of Robertson's investors, who requested anonymity, said that she could not believe all the bad press Robertson received for admitting to the losses. She also questioned whether the reporters really knew what they were talking about when they wrote stories on hedge funds.

"He had some losses, but he is also having a very good year," she said. "The press treats him unfairly because they don't understand what he does or how he does it. They also don't understand how he could be up so much when the mutual funds they themselves are investing in are not performing as well."

However, things were worse at Tiger than the public believed. On November 2, 1998, *The Wall Street Journal* ran a story titled "Robertson's Funds Become Paper Tigers as Blue October Leads to Red Ink for

'98." According to the story, the funds had lost over 17 percent or about $3.4 billion through October, which wiped out all of the funds' gains for the year. The funds' total losses through the end of October were approximately $5.5 billion, leaving Tiger with assets of around $17 billion, and it was expected to post losses of 3 percent for the month of November. By the middle of December the funds were down approximately 4 percent for the year.[2] On top of the losses the funds also faced a number of withdrawals from investors both in the United States and abroad. Although a number of industry watchers and observers seemed to believe that Tiger had significant amounts of withdrawals, the firm's public relations firm denied that this was the case. The spokesperson did say that the funds did have "some withdrawals but nothing significant."

Robertson's letter to investors seemed to be the only words of wisdom that investors, traders, and brokers could hold on to as the carnage in the hedge fund industry unfolded. Every day for four or five weeks the financial pages were filled with stories similar to the Robertson and Soros woes.

THE NEAR COLLAPSE OF LONG-TERM CAPITAL MANAGEMENT

Although the situation seemed dire as early as August, the financial community did not know what it was in for until September 21, 1998, when the news broke of the near collapse of a major hedge fund.

For weeks leading up to that Monday, there had been speculation that Long-Term Capital Management LP, a hedge fund with more than $3 billion in assets and run by one of Wall Street's smartest traders, was on the brink of collapse. Earlier in the summer, the firm had announced that it had lost over 44 percent of its assets. Rumors about it not being able to meet *margin calls* were running rampant through Wall Street.

The first real signs that something was dreadfully wrong came when the press broke a story that the New York Stock Exchange had launched an inquiry to determine if the fund was meeting its margin calls from brokers. There had been speculation that some of the brokers were giving Long-Term Capital special treatment and not making it meet its margin obligations, and the NYSE was trying to find out if it was true.

margin call   demand that an investor deposit enough money or securities to bring a margin account up to the minimum maintenance requirements.

Initially, things at the fund seemed to be under control. It was believed that its managers had put a stop to the hemorrhaging and were preserving the status quo. These rumors were part truth and part myth. Nobody on Wall Street—not the traders, not the brokers, and least of all the firms that had lent to Long-Term Capital—wanted to believe that it was in dire straits. This was not just some whiz kid trader who had just gotten out of business school and was flying by the seat of his pants. This was John Meriwether, the person who had invented and mastered the use of "rocket science" to make significant returns while limiting risk.

The fund was more than Meriwether; it was managed by some of the smartest minds around Wall Street's trading desks. At the time, Long-Term Capital's partners list read like a who's who of Wall Street's elite. People like Robert Merton and Myron Scholes, both Nobel economics laureates, as well as David Mullins, a former vice chairman of the Federal Reserve Board, were the people making trading decisions. And there were a number of former Salomon Brothers trading whizzes as well as a handful of Ph.D.s whom Meriwether had groomed personally.

How could this fund blow up? The question seemed ludicrous, especially because the market conditions that existed had often proved to be the ones in which this kind of fund thrived. Wall Street believed that it was impossible for Meriwether to be going the way of Victor Niederhoffer or David Askin—two other high-profile hedge fund managers who lost everything when funds they operated blew up in the mid-1990s.

Everyone, including himself, believed that Meriwether was the king of quants, as traders who use *quantitative analysis* and mathematics are called, a true master of the universe. People believed that the press had gotten things wrong and that of course the fund would be able to weather the storm.

quantitative analysis security analysis that uses objective statistical information to determine when to buy and sell securities.

"He has done it before," they said. "Of course he will do it again." Yet by the end of September 1998, there was one word to describe the previous statement: *wrong.*

The markets had gotten the best of Meriwether and his partners. He and his team of Ph.D.s and Nobel laureates had made mistakes that could not be reversed. They had bet the farm and then some and were on the brink of losing it all. The problem was a combination of leverage, risk, and, of course, greed—three ingredients that when mixed together come up with one thing: unsustainable losses.

The first news stories came out in late August and early September, after Meriwether announced in a letter to investors that the fund had lost a significant amount of assets. In his letter, which was subsequently published via Bloomberg News terminal, Meriwether blamed a number of circumstances for the losses. Still, he said, he and his colleagues and partners believed that the markets would turn in their favor; as long as they continued on the same path, investors would see light at the end of a very dark tunnel.

The letter stated, "Losses of this magnitude are a shock to us as they surely are to you," and that although the firm prided itself on its ability to post returns that are not correlated to the global bond, stock, or currency markets, too much happened too quickly for it to make things right. As with most of Meriwether's communications with investors, the letter did not delve into the types of trades or markets in which the fund was investing. The letter also did not discuss the amounts of leverage Long-Term Capital was using in its drive to capture enormous profits with even the slightest uptick. Nor did it explain that Meriwether had started to trade stock arbitrage positions, something completely different from the bond and currency plays with which he earned his stripes. The letter also failed to mention that the fund had just borrowed money from itself to cover its operating expenses.

The simplest explanation of what happened to Long-Term Capital is that because financial crises hit in more than one market simultaneously, there were no profitable situations in the multiple markets in which it had placed trades. Basically, everything that could have gone wrong did. Although the firm specialized in finding unique situations regardless of the condition of the market, and employed many "if, then" scenarios, the one thing the partners never were able to figure out was what to do if everything they planned for happened at the same time. The strength of Long-Term Capital's operation rested on the managers' ability to determine what would happen to the prices of many securities when various events hit the market, but their black boxes never told them what would occur if everything they thought possible happened at the same time.

For example, it was widely reported that the fund was short U.S. Treasuries and long high-yield paper and other risky illiquid investments. The idea was that as Treasury prices fell, yields would increase and the other types of debt instruments would rise in price.

The exact opposite happened. When the turmoil hit the markets, there was an immediate flight to quality, resulting in a significant increase in Treasury prices and a significant decrease in prices of riskier investments. Instead of converging, the trade diverged and ended up going in the wrong direction on both sides of the ticket. When prices of

Treasuries shoot up, the yield goes down, and likewise when the prices of high-yield debt go down, the yield increases. Markets that were illiquid to begin with became even more illiquid, and the Treasury market, which has enormous liquidity at all times, showed its lowest yields in a generation.

To understand how the firm could have lost so much so quickly and supposedly even put the world markets at great risk, one first needs to understand how Long-Term Capital operated. The firm specialized in bond arbitrage, a trading strategy Meriwether mastered while working at Salomon Brothers in the 1980s. Traders, using very complex mathematical formulas, capitalize on small price discrepancies among securities in various markets. The idea is to exploit the prices of certain bonds by buying or selling the security based on the perceived value, not the current market value. Meriwether pioneered the use of these strategies while he worked at Salomon. When Wall Streeters found out that it worked, they called it rocket science, because it was so complex.

The idea behind Long-Term Capital from its outset was to employ these strategies to capture significant profits while enjoying insignificant amounts of risk. Meriwether and his partners were not interested in making a killing on a single trade but rather in picking up small amounts with relatively minor swings in the market from multiple trades. The idea was to employ enough leverage that even the slightest market movement would cause the firm to profit quite handsomely.

If they bought a stock at $100, they would not wait for it to go to $120 or $180 but rather would sell out when it hit $101. Making a dollar does not seem like much, but because their leverage was in excess of 20 to 1 they were able to make big profits on the very small (1 percent) movement. With $100 of equity, the fund would have been able to control $2,000 worth of stock. So in this hypothetical situation, the profit would have been approximately 20 percent. If a $100 investment leveraged at 20 to 1 goes up 10 percent, the trade yields a $200 profit, or a yield of 200 percent on the initial $100, a tripling in value.[3]

In the aftermath of the fund's meltdown, there was of course a lot of Monday morning quarterbacking with very little explanation of what went wrong. *The New York Times* managed to get some unique color on the situation:

> As one Salomon Brothers veteran described it, [Meriwether's] fund was like a roulette player betting on red and doubling up its bets each time the wheel stopped on black. "A gambler with $1,000 will probably lose," he said. "A gambler with $1 billion will wind up owning the casino, because it is a mathematical certainty that red will come up eventually—but you have to have enough chips to stay at the table until that happens."[4]

One thing for sure is that to stay at the table, Meriwether used significant amounts of leverage. The problem was that at Long-Term Capital, leverage got out of hand.

The first indication that things had taken a turn for the worse was in July 1998. Meriwether announced that the fund had posted a loss of some $300 million for the month of June. It was first time the fund had posted a loss for a month since its inception four years earlier. Reports at the time questioned the veil of secrecy that surrounded the fund's trading and it was unclear where the losses were coming from. The fund had operated in complete silence when it came to discussing strategy or positions, because it believed that once people understood where it was making money, they could determine where its next moves would be and copy its strategies. Very few outside Meriwether's inner circle knew what markets the fund was trading in and where profits and losses originated.

Initial reports had the losses coming from the turmoil that rocked the mortgage-backed securities markets. Still, because of the size of the losses, people suspected that the firm had losses elsewhere, including the currency and U.S. Treasuries markets.

It was quite a shock to many on Wall Street when the losses were announced. For years, Long-Term Capital had performed extremely well and its leader was considered to be too smart to make mistakes. Many others could make mistakes and fail but not John Meriwether and his quants. Wall Street believed that these men and women walked on water. The firm perpetuated the myth time and time again by putting up strong returns, no matter what the condition of the market.

In 1995, the firm was up over 42 percent, net of fees, while in 1996 and 1997 it was up 41 percent and 17 percent respectively. Long-Term Capital did not just beat the averages; it trounced them.

Still, never would the statement "Past performance is no indication of future results" become more pertinent than during the summer of 1998.

On a very hot day in August, a person I was interviewing for this book told me that Long-Term Capital's losses for June were just the tip of the iceberg; that the firm had sustained enormous losses the previous Friday when buyers dumped corporate bonds and bought Treasuries, sending yields to their lowest point in 20 years. The person told me that a friend had just come from a meeting with a New York investor who said he was pulling out of Long-Term Capital and that Meriwether was on the verge of bankruptcy. I was shocked. On my way out of the interview, I immediately called friends at New York newspapers to try the story. It was possible that other superstars had blown up and of course many smaller hedge funds run by inexperienced managers have failed. But not Long-Term Capital! Its managers were the best and brightest that Wall Street had to offer next to George Soros, Julian Robertson, Michael Steinhardt, and Paul Tudor Jones.

Nobody that morning could confirm the story but by mid-afternoon I did get in touch with someone who echoed my interviewee's statements. Long-Term had posted significant losses.

The next day a number of stories appeared in the papers confirming that Meriwether had lost a significant amount and that the fund needed a large capital infusion to stay afloat. Things looked quite grim for the Midas traders of Greenwich, Connecticut.

It was the first indication that September was going to be a very long month for Long-Term Capital's management and investors, its trading partners, and the entire hedge fund industry.

The story came out because someone leaked a letter that Meriwether had written to investors explaining the situation and requesting new capital. He asked that investors be patient and that they supply him with new capital to "take full advantage of this unusually attractive environment."

People who spoke with him about the letter explained that he believed that by attracting new capital, he would be able to put a hold on the losses and be able to take advantage of the inevitable turnaround that was about to come.

"By continuing to employ strategies that had worked in the past, John believed he would be able to recover from this dreadful situation," a hedge fund manager who is close to Meriwether said. "The problem was people had lost faith. Never had the statement 'you're only as good as your last trade' been more prevalent on Wall Street."

Acknowledgment of the problem came a little too late to stop the hemorrhaging. By the time Meriwether asked for more money, the losses were too great. Even if investors had decided to pony up the extra dollars, they would have only been able to stave off the inevitable for a little while because the need for cash was so great. The well had dried up and the opportunities, it seemed, no longer existed.

At the time he wrote to investors, Meriwether probably did not have any idea where the money to bail out his firm would come from nor the extent of what the bailout would cost. Besides looking for capital from his investors, Meriwether approached outsiders, including Warren Buffett and George Soros, all of whom turned him down.

Buffett did resurface, but as a potential purchaser of the operation, not as an investor. He along with Goldman Sachs Group LP and American International Group Inc. offered to buy the entire operation from Meriwether and to assume the fund's massive portfolios. Meriwether said no, because he did not want to give up control. The press seemed to believe that Meriwether's ego had gotten in the way of getting the deal done with Buffett.

On Monday, September 21, 1998, Wall Street's most powerful and influential players got calls from representatives of the Federal Reserve Bank of New York. Some of the recipients were surprised that the Fed was going to intervene in a situation over which it had no direct control. Because of the structure of hedge funds, they are not regulated by either the Fed or the Securities and Exchange Commission (SEC) and are basically free to operate without any regulatory supervision.

The president of the New York Fed requested that Wall Street's elite meet to discuss the fate of one of its own. Not since the days of J. P. Morgan had such a group of Wall Street moguls assembled in one room with the intention of devising a plan to save an institution as well as possibly themselves.

Initially, people credited the New York Fed as the stimulus for the bailout, but subsequent reports credited John Corzine, co-managing partner at Goldman Sachs, as the person who got the ball rolling. Still, it is believed that the Fed prompted him after it started questioning the amount of money Long-Term Capital owed companies under its supervision. It has been suggested that both Goldman Sachs and Merrill Lynch & Co. Inc. had been on the brink of losing so much money because of Long-Term Capital's inability to pay that the Federal Reserve was worried that other firms might themselves be pushed to the brink of insolvency should it go bankrupt. Unlike other bankruptcies, when hedge funds go out of business all of their positions are liquidated immediately, in most cases at fire sale prices. It is unknown exactly how much money was at stake, but it is clear that trillions of dollars would have been wiped out if there had been a forced liquidation.

It was also clear that the fund had come to the end of its rope. It needed money to meet its margin obligations or else havoc would reign over the world's already tumultuous markets. For the first time in a very long time the Fed had determined that an organization was "too big to fail," and it was going to do everything in its power to ensure that it did not fail.

Did the Fed do the right thing? The people I spoke with seemed divided on the issue. Although the debate will go on for some time, one thing is for sure: In light of the takeover by the consortium, Long-Term Capital was able to right itself and started earning money again in the fourth quarter of 1998.

The Federal Reserve had hoped that Goldman Sachs would find

a buyer for the fund, but when that failed, it asked the dozen or so companies to come up with a workable solution to this very serious problem.

When the announcement was made that the potential buyer had walked, David Komansky, chairman of Merrill Lynch, took over the discussion to determine to what extent the companies would contribute to keep Long-Term Capital alive and possibly keep a number of themselves from collapsing as well.

By all accounts, a number balked but quickly realized that they had to act together. In the end, 14 companies decided to contribute to the bailout, committing sums ranging from $100 million to $350 million. One that did not participate was Bear Stearns & Co., Inc. It was agreed that it should not chip in to the bailout because its risk as Long-Term Capital's clearing broker significantly outweighed the risk posed to other contributors. Table 1.1 illustrates to what extent each company contributed to the bailout.

TABLE 1.1 Bailout of Long-Term Capital Management	
$100 Million	*$300 Million*
Banque Parlbas	Bankers Trust
Crédit Agricole	Barclays
Lehman Brothers	Chase Manhattan
	Credit Suisse First Boston
$125 Million	Deutsche Bank
Société Générale	Goldman Sachs
	JP Morgan
	Merrill Lynch
	Morgan Stanley
	Salomon Smith Barney
	Union Bank of Switzerland

Source: The Wall Street Journal, November 16, 1998.

Although because of the secrecy surrounding the operation it is unclear who lost what, it is apparent that many of Wall Street's most important executives took some very big hits when the firm went down. The rescue plan reduced all of the investors' stakes to under 10 percent of what they had been. Executives of some of Wall Street's most prestigious companies—including Merrill Lynch, Bear Stearns, and PaineWebber Group Inc.—faced personal losses. A number of partners at the famed consulting firm McKinsey & Co. lost money as well.

The irony of the situation is that in the wake of the collapse, *The Wall Street Journal, The New York Times,* and *The New York Post* all reported that a number of investors were quite happy that earlier in 1998 Long-Term Capital had returned money to them. Yet most investors who received money back were quite upset at the time. In December 1997, Long-Term Capital had returned approximately $2.7 billion to investors ranging from small money managers to PaineWebber and the Bank of China.

The only firm on Wall Street that seemed to have done well with Long-Term Capital was PaineWebber.[5] It and its chairman and chief executive, Donald Marron, had invested $100 million and $10 million in the fund respectively. Both, however, received money back in 1997. According to a number of reports, the firm more than doubled its investment and Marron got enough money back at least to break even.

Other Wall Streeters were not so lucky. Bear Stearns chief executive James Cayne and executive vice president Warren Spector are believed to have lost more than $9 million each. Merrill Lynch's Komansky, who along with over a hundred of his colleagues had invested approximately $22 million in the fund, saw that position reduced to less than $2 million once the bailout was complete.

The idea that a hedge fund got too big to fail is quite remarkable. By the time the bailout agreement was reached, Long-Term Capital had received commitments in excess of $3.5 billion to be used to meet margin calls and to cover operating expenses. The bailout was designed to ensure that the firm would not collapse and cause credit markets around the world to cave in from the dumping of all of the securities. It is believed that if the fund had been forced to liquidate, it might have caused the undermining of more than $1 trillion in assets.

This experience makes it quite clear that the bull market of the mid- and late 1990s had gotten out of control and once again an enormous level of greed had come over the Street. The only way Long-Term Capital was able to become so large was that it was lent money without any regard for whether it could pay back what it borrowed. The lenders looked instead to the fees associated with the transactions and the continuous stream of revenue the firm would provide to line the brokerages' and banks' pockets. In the end, all the lenders risked losing more than they had bargained for—their own existence. It is this that has probably put everything back in perspective.

In the wake of the Long-Term Capital disaster, the calls for hedge fund reform and regulation swept the nation and the world. Congress held hearings and industry observers cried foul, but, in the wake of the scandal and impeachment that rocked the White House, hedge funds took a backseat. Nothing came of the hearings and no new regulations were put in place.

The New York Times reported that one Wall Street executive who was briefed on the negotiations that led to the bailout said that he had learned a lesson about his own firm's operation after reviewing its exposure to Long-Term Capital.

"We will never let our exposure to one counterparty get to these levels again—never. He had gotten too big for the market," he said of Meriwether. "Everybody gave him too much money."[6] That is of course the case until another Midas trader hits the Street.

A few months later, however, things had started to turn around for Long-Term Capital Management and Meriwether. First the hedge fund reported profits and then came the speculation the fund was looking to buy out its saviors and that if an amicable arrangement could not be met, Meriwether would start a new investment vehicle. While the buyout never seemed to materialize, the fund's financial situation had completely turned around by the Spring of 1999. Meriwether and his partners had paid back a significant portion of the bailout and had started talking about a new fund that they planned on launching.

In the early fall, Long-Term Capital had paid back close to 75 percent of the bailout to the consortium of financial institutions that had saved it a year earlier. The consortium issued a statement at the end of September stating that "the portfolio is in excellent shape" and that risk profile of the fund had been reduced by nearly 90 percent. One of the stipulations of the bailout was that before the Long-Term Capital's managers could operate a new fund, they had to repay 90 percent of the money the banks put into it. This meant that the fund needed to repay an additional $600 million to the consortium before Meriwether and his partners could raise money for a new fund. A spokesman for the consortium said that it expected to be completely paid back by the end of the first quarter of the year 2000.

"Long-Term Capital Management is close to being out of business," said William McDonough, president of the Federal Reserve Bank of New York. "All of the banks that re-capitalized it have gotten most of their money back from the fund."

Meriwether would not comment on the status of the new fund; however, industry sources said he expected to be operating it by November 2000 with approximately $1 billion under management and that it was going to be called JWM Partners.

A BRIEF HISTORY OF HEDGE FUNDS

It used to be that if you queried students at business schools about where they wanted to work after graduation, responses would be names like Salomon Brothers, Goldman Sachs, or Morgan Stanley as well as General Motors, Coca-Cola, or IBM.

Now, however, students say they want to work for firms like Omega Advisors, Tiger Management, and Soros Fund Management—in other words, hedge funds, organizations that were not on the radar screen of Middle America until the near collapse of Long-Term Capital. Still, on Wall Street these firms have always been looked at with awe.

Once considered a small and obscure pocket of the Street, these firms represent one of the fastest-growing areas of the financial world.

Because of their nature, hedge funds are supposed to thrive regardless of market conditions.

To understand how the hedge fund industry evolved one needs first to understand where the concept came from. Let's define what a hedge fund is and how it works.

The term was coined by Alfred Winslow Jones, a sociologist, author, and financial journalist who got interested in the markets while writing about stocks for *Fortune* magazine in the 1940s.

Jones started the first known hedge fund in 1949 and as such defined the term by his style of investing, management, and organizational structure.

Although Jones is credited with laying the foundation for the industry, many on Wall Street believe Roy Neuberger, the founder of the securities firm Neuberger Berman, Inc., was the person who created the concept of a hedge fund. And there are others who believe it was Benjamin Graham, the father of securities analysis, who devised the method and formula for paying managers.

Regardless, when people think of the history of hedge funds and where they came from, they always think of Alfred Winslow Jones.

The problem is that many do not know about the Jones organization or his investment style or how he defined his hedge fund. In fact, there had not been an article of substance written about Jones for more than 20 years until October 1998, when *Grant's Interest Rate Observer* published a significant story on Jones in the wake of the near collapse of Long-Term Capital.

The industry has changed quite substantially since Jones launched his fund, A. W. Jones & Co. The most important change is to the definition of what he created.

Today the popular press defines hedge funds as private investment pools of money that wealthy individuals, families, and institutions invest in to protect assets and to achieve rates of return above and in fact well beyond those offered by mutual funds or other investment opportunities. For the most part, the press is correct. Where it errs is in defining the methodology as well as the concept of these private investment vehicles for sophisticated investors.

We'll discuss later the intricacies of the way hedge funds operate as well as just who invests in them and why. The term "hedge fund" is like most things on Wall Street—it sounds tricky but once it is dissected it is quite easy to understand.

It is my belief from talking to colleagues, relatives, and friends of Jones that he had no intention of creating a difficult product. Rather, I believe he would have wanted the masses to understand his idea of the use of hedges to minimize risk and hoped that it would be employed more widely throughout the investing world.

One of the reasons hedge funds were obscure until the Long-Term Capital debacle is the way the press describes their trading operations and styles. Reporters seem to be afraid of scratching more than the surface, but truly enjoy using the term for shock purposes in news stories with headlines like "Soros Loses $2 Billion in Russia" or "Robertson's Tiger Pounces."

These are simple words that grab attention with little or no explanation of the operation. It is not all the fault of the press in most cases, since hedge fund managers hide behind Securities and Exchange Commission rules regarding marketing and solicitation. The SEC does not allow managers to market their funds or to solicit investors that are not prequalified, and talking to the press could be construed as marketing. Still, the information usually gets out and I believe it would do the industry good if managers were a little less tight-lipped.

I will say, as I wrote in the acknowledgment section of this book, that for the most part everyone I asked to talk about their own business and the industry spoke freely and I believe honestly. Also, in the past year or so, in light of a number of financial crises, it seems managers are opening up more. This, in my opinion, can only help the industry.

In the 50 years since the hedge fund industry evolved, only three articles have been written about the subject that have any real merit or worth. Two are by the same journalist and ran in *Fortune* magazine, while the third was published in *Institutional Investor.*

To understand how important the articles are to the industry, we first need to understand the Jones model. It is very simple to follow and is the most accurate definition of a hedge fund. No matter how far managers today deviate from the definition, each and every one operates with some of Jones's original characteristics.

According to Jones, as described by Carol Loomis in her January 1970 article in *Fortune* titled "Hard Times Come to the Hedge Funds" (still considered to be one of the definitive articles on Jones and the industry), a hedge fund is a *limited partnership* structured so as to give the general partners—the managers—a share of the profits earned on the limited partners' money. Further, a hedge fund always uses leverage and always carries some short positions. Jones called his investment vehicle a "hedged fund"—a fund that is hedged and is protected against market swings by the structure of its long and short positions. Somewhere along the line Wall Street's powers that be dropped off the "d."

limited partnership a legal term used to describe the structure of most hedge funds and private investment vehicles.

The method for sharing in the profits is defined in the hedge fund's fee structure. Under the Jones scenario, the managers receive 20 percent of the portfolio's profits—and nothing else. Therefore they have quite an incentive to pick winners.

In recent years, managers have added a *management fee* of 1 to 1.5 percent of assets to the 20 percent *performance fee*. It is unclear who decided to add this fee, but like most things on Wall Street, when it works people copy it. This fee basically allows the managers to cover the cost of maintaining the fund's operations as well as providing a bit of a salary. The Jones organization never levied management fees on its partners.

management fee fee paid to the manager for day-to-day operation of the hedge fund.

performance fee   fee paid to manager based on how well the investment strategy performs.

According to Robert Burch, Jones's son-in-law and the current operator of A. W. Jones & Co., Jones never believed in management fees.

"He believed that [management fees] would only breed more assets and take away from the concept of performance and induce the fact that you could make more money building assets than through performing according to the model," says Burch. "Jones was concerned with performance and did not want to be distracted by asset-gathering."

For the most part, the Jones model worked well in both up and down markets, as it was intended to do. In its first 20 years of operation, the system worked so well that the Jones fund never had a losing year. It was not until the bear market of the late 1960s and 1970 that it posted losses.

The hedge fund industry has truly grown very large very fast. It seems that everyone who wants to be in the money management business wants to work for or own a hedge fund. This is not theory but practice, as many mutual fund managers, traders, and analysts are jumping ship to start their own funds. These people are setting up entities that they call a hedge fund and—voilà!—they are in the business.

The problem is that many who are calling themselves hedge fund managers are not. To have a hedge fund you have to *hedge*. Therefore, those who do not hedge but call themselves a hedge fund are operating nothing more than a very expensive mutual fund.

Many managers still follow the classical Jones model, using leverage and having long and short positions that allow you to maximize returns while limiting risks in both rising and falling markets. Probably the person who best exemplifies the Jones model today is Julian Robertson.

Robertson, who will be discussed in Chapter 2, is considered by most to be the person who took over Jones's spot as the dean of the hedge fund industry. Although his fund organization is not the largest, and it operates in relative obscurity, it is Robertson who best exemplifies what Jones had in mind when he defined and developed his idea.

Robertson, who covered Jones while he worked at Kidder Peabody, has built an enormously successful business, at one time managing in excess of $20 billion. Like most other hedge fund managers, Robertson lost a considerable amount of money in the turmoil of 1998—more than 10 percent of his assets under management. He is known to be an arrogant, egomaniacal hard worker who is possibly the greatest money manager of all time.

"Julian is the natural successor to Jones," says Burch. "He has built a business around the principles and disciplines that Jones used to build his business. He understands the Jones model and uses it to make superior returns regardless of market conditions."

THE CURRENT STATE OF THE HEDGE FUND INDUSTRY

It is impossible to get an absolute number of how many hedge funds exist or the exact amount of assets the industry as a whole has under management. The numbers of both change as fast as you can make telephone calls to people who track this information. The Securities and Exchange Commission requires mutual funds and corporations to report financial information to it quarterly, which makes these data literally just a click away.

With hedge funds it is not so easy. There is no regulation or requirement for fund managers to report data. Many fund managers are quite happy reporting data when profits are up; but as soon as things go south, the information does not flow so freely. Often, a fund manager also ignores the tracking companies when the fund reaches investor capacity and can no longer accept investment dollars from outside its current group of investors. In this case, the fund manager no longer needs the tracking service, because new investors will only have to be turned away. The only time partners actually get an accounting of the industry is when a fund or funds blow up. And even those numbers need to be questioned because the legal issues do not require a total accounting to be made public.

For the purposes of this book, I am going to define the size and scope of the industry as follows: There are 3,000 hedge funds with $500 billion under management, a 300-fold growth in less than 30 years.

In 1971, an SEC report on institutional investors estimated that hedge funds had $1.06 billion under management.[7] At the time, the SEC found that Alfred Winslow Jones's organization had just under 23 percent of all of the assets under management placed with hedge funds.[8]

Today, a hedge fund can be any sort of private investment vehicle that is created as either a limited partnership or a limited liability corporation. In either case, the vehicle falls under very narrow SEC and Internal Revenue Service (IRS) rules and regulations. It is limited as to how many investors it can have, either 100 or 500 depending on its structure. The structure also determines the type of investors it can accept, either accredited or super-accredited.[9] Institutions that include nonfinancial companies are able to invest in either type of fund.

In light of the hedge fund debacle of 1998, Congress and other United States officials have been pressing for more controls and monitoring systems for the industry. As of yet, nothing has come from their cries for help. Many believe that nothing ever will because if you have enough money to invest in a hedge fund you do not need to have your hand held by the government.

The reason many of Wall Street's Midas traders and would-be Midas traders are flocking to set up and work for hedge funds is because it is what some consider the last bastion of capitalism.

"When we started, it was very difficult to get through the paperwork and raise capital," says Jim Rogers, who was George Soros's partner for more than 10 years. "Now it is very easy and people specialize in setting up the funds and raising capital. It is probably the most efficient way to make money in the financial world."

Rogers's sentiments are echoed in an article about hedge funds that appeared in the June 8, 1998, issue of *Fortune* magazine. The article described a number of start-up funds and their managers. Why did they leave their soft jobs at white-shoe investment firms to go out on their own? The answers: freedom and money.

According to the article, written by Bethany McLean, "No other career in finance gives you the freedom to be your own boss and invest in anything, anywhere, that gets your juices flowing," or provides these people with the opportunity to "get so rich, so fast, so young."[10]

McLean quoted one manager's quip: "I can wager your money on the Knicks game if I want."[11] This is true, it is legal, and it is very, very scary.

A number of former Jones employees have said that many of these people would not have been able to work for their company nor to succeed in the markets in which the Jones organization thrived. Clearly statements like the one above were not what Jones had in mind when he developed hedge funds.

Still, to understand this and where the idea of a hedge fund came from as well as how the business was born, one needs to learn about the father of it all.

ALFRED WINSLOW JONES—THE ORIGINAL HEDGE FUND MANAGER

Alfred Winslow Jones started what has come to be known as the first hedge fund in 1949. His basic investment strategy was to use leverage in combination with long and short sales in order to hedge risk should the market turn against him.

Jones, who died at the age of 88 in June of 1989, devised a formula for the vehicle while researching a freelance article for *Fortune* titled "Fashion in Forecasting," which ran in the March 1949 issue. To research the piece, he spent many hours speaking with some of Wall Street's great traders and brokers. Upon learning their methods, he devised his own ideas on investing based around the concept of hedging—something very few people did in those days. And so with three partners he launched the fund at the age of 49.

"My father took a very long time to find himself," says Anthony Jones, one of Jones's two children. "He graduated from college with some of the same loose ends that many people who graduate have today and basically tried a number of things before he realized what he wanted to do."

After traveling the world on a tramp steamer as purser, he believed he had found himself when he joined the Foreign Service.

"He was in Germany in the early thirties and watched the rise of Hitler and then was assigned to Venezuela, and the prospect of going from Berlin to Venezuela was so depressing that he quit the Foreign Service," Tony Jones says. "He came to the United States and got involved in sociology."

Jones's interests in sociology and the idea of how social movements developed led him to enter Columbia University. He earned a Ph.D. in sociology in 1941, and it was at Columbia where he met Benjamin Graham.

"His graduate work was interrupted by my parents' marriage and their honeymoon took them to civil war Spain," says Tony Jones. "In Spain they did a survey for the Quakers—neither of them carried a rifle or drove an ambulance—and toured around with interesting people reporting on civilian relief."

Upon returning to the United States, Jones took a job with *Fortune,* where he worked until 1946. Whether he knew it or not, it was here where he would be laying the groundwork for a lifetime career.

After leaving *Fortune,* he worked as a freelancer for it and other magazines, writing on social and political issues as well as finance. The research and reporting Jones did for "Fashion in Forecasting" convinced him that working on Wall Street was not as difficult as many believed.

"He would come home every day while he was reporting the piece and tell me that he did not learn anything new," recalled his widow, Mary. "After a while he started working on an idea and finally came up with something he believed would work." Mary Jones died on January 8, 1999, at the age of 91.

The article looked at how stock market behavior was interpreted by technicians of statistics, charts, and trends. The following is an excerpt of the piece.

> The standard, old-fashioned method of predicting the course of the stock market is first to look at facts and figures external to the market itself, and then examine stock prices to see whether they are too high or too low. Freight-car loadings, commodity prices, bank clearings, the outlook for tax legislation, political prospects, the danger of war, and countless other factors determine corporations' earnings and dividends, and these, combined with money rates, are supposed to (and in the long run do) determine the prices of common stocks. But in the meantime awkward things get in the way (and in the long run, as Keynes said, we shall be dead).
>
> In the late summer of 1946, for instance, the Dow Jones industrial stock average dropped in five weeks from 205 to 163, part of the move to a minor panic. In spite of the stock market, business was good before the break, remained good through it, and has been good ever since.
>
> Nevertheless there are market analysts, whose concern is the internal character of the market, who could see the decline coming. To get these predictive powers they study the statistics that the stock market itself grinds out day after day. Refined, manipulated in various ways, and interpreted, these data are sold by probably as many as twenty stock-market services and are used independently by hundreds, perhaps thousands, of individuals. They are increasingly used by brokerage firms, by some because the users believe in them and by others because their use brings in business.[12]

"I was a young kid at the time the business was started, and I have no recollection of when he stopped going to work at *Fortune* or writing and started going to work for himself," says Tony Jones. "I do have quite fond memories of going to visit him at his office down at 80 Broad Street in the heart of Wall Street."

Jones's model for his fund had a very simple formula. He basically used leverage and short sales to create a system that allowed him to concentrate on stock picking rather than market timing.

According to Tony Jones, he realized very early on that he was not a good stock picker. Indeed, Tony Jones believes that it was this realization that led him to expand the organization, bringing in budding Wall Street stars to run the partnership's money, to the point where it became successful.

"He was a good salesman; he knew people to raise money from, and was a good organizer and administrator. But when it came to picking stocks, he had no particular talent," he says. "This meant that his job was to find people who did have talent."

Working for and with the Jones organization was very lucrative. All partners received a piece of the 20 percent that Jones was paid by the limited partners and they were able to invest in the vehicle.

Brokers knew that if they had an idea and the Jones people liked it, they could sell it over the phone. One broker told me that he used to like to run all of his ideas by the Jones people before calling other clients. He knew that they would act immediately if they liked his idea, but also would tell him if the situation would not work and in turn helped him from pushing a bad stock.

"These were some of the smartest and savviest investors and traders of the time," the broker says. "They gave you a straight scoop on the situation. It was a lot of fun covering the account."

Besides developing the hedge fund, the Jones organization perfected the art of paying brokers to give up ideas. Although the firm executed most of its orders through Neuberger Berman, Inc., it paid brokers for ideas. Should a broker call on one of Jones's managers, he knew that if the manager used his idea, he would be paid regardless of where the order was executed.

"When Jones's people got an idea, they would call us and execute the order and tell us where the idea came from," remembers Roy Neuberger. "We would give up half of the commission to the guy who came up with the idea, whether he worked for us or not. At the time I did not think the exchange would let us do it. But they did, no ifs, ands, or buts; it was perfectly all right with them."

Neuberger continues, "For many years, the Jones account was the firm's most important account. But it was more than business. We were friends; both he and his wife were friends of my wife and me, and we socialized together."

Jones's strength seemed to be in people as well as ideas. His organization gave birth to many successful managers.

"There were a whole bunch of people who used to work for my father that went on their own," recalls Tony Jones. "After a while he began a business of farming the money out and created a sort of hedge fund of hedge funds."

A number of Jones alumni are still in the business to this day, including Walter Harrison, Banks Adams, and Ron Labow.

"Jones made no attempt to pick stocks; he was an executive," says Neuberger. "He understood how to get things done and how to find people to execute his ideas."

One former Jones employee told me that the hardest part of working for Jones was actually getting the invitation to work for him. Jones used a number of techniques to tell the good from the bad, one of which was a paper portfolio program.

"In order to work for my father you first had to prove yourself," Tony Jones says. "To prove yourself, you needed to manage a play portfolio of stocks over a period of, say, six months or so. Every day, you had to call in your trades to the firm and they would be 'executed.' It was only after my father was able to watch how the manager was doing with the play money that he invited them in as partners."

The firm tallied up the profits and losses and examined not only how well the prospective managers performed but also how they did it.

"When it came to hiring managers, my father was very cautious," Tony Jones says. "He wanted to know how they operated and watched very carefully to see what types of decisions they made with the play money. If everything worked out, they got a job."

Another interesting point of the Jones organization was that he did not fire people. If you performed poorly, he simply did not give you any more money to manage and took pieces away little by little so eventually there was nothing left. And the manager had to leave.

From all accounts, Jones was very satisfied and proud of his invention and he appreciated the publicity that he received. Yet he was not very interested in talking about money or the stock market.

"Jones was not a man who was very interested in Wall Street or making money; rather he was interested in the intellectual challenge of it all," says son-in-law Burch. "Although he made a lot of money, he was not very interested in spending and gave a lot of his money away, creating things like the Reverse Peace Corps and other foundations to help people here in the United States."

Jones was very involved with a number of charitable organizations in New York City. One cause to which he was a major contributor and in which his son and daughter are still quite active is the Henry Street Settlement.

Founded in 1893 by Lillian Wald on Manhattan's Lower East Side, the Henry Street Settlement provides programs that range from transitional residences for homeless families and a mental health clinic to a senior services center and a community arts center.

"My father liked to travel to Third World countries. He liked to have a mission, but he had a notion that a number of nations criticized the United States for not doing enough to help out on their own shores and that drew him to Henry Street," remembers Dale Burch, Jones's daughter. "He liked the fact that it helped the community from within itself."

Jones also created an operation called Globalization for Youth, an antipoverty program that used a number of resources to keep children from getting into trouble.

"These are types of things we talked about," says Tony Jones. "He was very concerned with family solidarity and all of the theories that evolved in the late fifties and early sixties that are currently social work orthodoxy."

Once he launched his fund he very rarely talked about what he did or how he did it. "When you had dinner with Jones, you always had four or five guys from various parts of the world," recalls Burch. "You didn't know if that night you were going to discuss some pending revolt in Albania or what language they were speaking in Iran.

"It was an interesting challenge to participate in the dinner conversation. The discussion was never about money and never about Wall Street—his mind was way beyond that," he continues.

Tony Jones recalls that when the family went to their country home in Connecticut, his mother would drive and his father would go through the evening newspaper with a list of all the stocks his managers had and calculate how they had done that day.

That was the extent to which he brought the business home.

"There was absolutely no time for discussions of what stocks might go up or down at home," says Tony Jones.

Jones did not have many of the characteristics of other Wall Street legends. For example, according to his son, at Christmastime when the brokerages his firm did business with wanted to give him presents, he would accept only items that could be consumed.

"Many of the Wall Street firms tried desperately to give him gifts as a thank-you for all of the revenue he generated, and he would never accept anything except for something he could eat in the next week," Tony Jones recollects. "We got a Christmas turkey from Neuberger Berman but when it came to gold cuff links or the like, forget about it."

Roy Neuberger called Jones a thinker, not necessarily a hard worker, a sentiment that seems to be echoed by his son.

"My father's entire life was preoccupied with ideas, some crazy and some not so crazy," Tony Jones says. "He had the capacity to read a book and then just get on the phone and call the author up and have lunch. He got to know people and many things and was constantly thinking about everything under the sun."

According to Tony Jones, after his father read a book claiming that the works of Shakespeare had been written by the 16th Earl of Oxford, he decided that the theory was sound and talked about it for two years.

"After his journalism days, and getting in the business, he did not really have long-term interests," Tony Jones says. "He was more interested in things he could focus on short-term. The idea of tackling big projects was not something he was interested in."

Besides countless articles, Jones did publish one book, *Life, Liberty, and Property,* in 1941, based on his doctoral dissertation. According to Daniel Nelson, a history professor at the University of Akron, it was the rarest of dissertations: technically sophisticated, engaging, and addressed to a general audience. A new edition of the book was published in March 1999 by the University of Akron Press.

Although most of the articles written about Jones say he had planned to write a second book, his son says he wanted to but "it would have been a monumental task." When Jones retired from the hedge fund business completely in 1982, he was satisfied with the business but not with its being his life's work.

"Later on in his life, he wanted to write a memoir but could not focus himself on getting it done," Tony Jones says. "There was nothing about running his business that required real concentration—it was a brainstorm kind of thing and he was good at it."

Jones did not simply hit an age and retire. Rather, he started to give up his duties at the firm and eventually turned the reins over to Lester Kissel. Kissel, a lawyer from the firm Seward & Kissel and an original partner in A. W. Jones & Co., assumed control for a few years. Because of conflicts over the direction of the organization, he was asked to step down and after a brief stint by Jones, Burch took over.

"My father was not at the top of his game when he turned things over to Kissel," says Tony Jones. "Kissel was a lawyer, not a businessman. He never did anything intentionally to harm my father but he did hurt the business."

By today's standards, Jones did not become extraordinarily wealthy from the business. Still, he spent the bulk of the money he did have on charities, not on lavish living.

However, one of Jones's great loves was his 200-acre estate in Connecticut that allowed him to enjoy the outdoors.

"My father was a landscape visionary," says his son. "He was always trying to figure out things to do with water and moving land around.

"His mind was all over the place," he continues. "Everything he did, did not require an enormous amount of steady follow-through on his part. He had a lot of good ideas and made them reality."

Tony Jones believes his father's reason for switching from journalism to Wall Street was that he wanted to live comfortably and he knew that he could not achieve that as a journalist.

"He had carved out a unique niche for himself writing but realized that he would never be able to live the kind of lifestyle he wanted to being a journalist," says Tony Jones. "My father was also determined to find out if his crazy idea would work."

Although most people point to the research for the *Fortune* article as the genesis, a number I talked to seem to think a combination of things led him to the hedge fund concept.

It is quite clear that while Jones was studying at Columbia he had many conversations with Graham and learned investing strategies from him. This may be where the seeds of the idea were planted.

Jones did know another Graham follower, Warren Buffett, and the two lunched together from time to time.

"The principles of the hedge fund were clearly developed and created by Alfred. However, some of his investment strategies may have come from his discussions with Buffett and Graham," says Burch. "He was the first to put the ideas down on paper and then actually put them to use."

Jones defined the principles of hedge funds as follows:

1. You had to be short all the time.

2. You always use leverage.

3. The manager receives a fee of 20 percent of all profits.

"It was the combinations of shorting, the use of leverage, and the fee structure, which is how Jones defined what a hedge fund was all about," says Burch.

Jones believed that by aggressively picking long stocks and neutralizing market swings by also being short, he would be able to put up extraordinary performance numbers while reducing risks.

39

At all times, Jones's funds maintained a number of short positions that would enable them to have a hedge against a drop in the market, which limited his downside exposure. It is impossible to get a complete accounting of the fund's track record because of the private nature of its activities and investors.

According to *The New York Times* obituary, in the 10 years prior to 1968 the firm had posted gains up to 1,000 percent. It is estimated that the Jones fund had over $200 million under management at the end of that period.

Soon after that, however, things began to not go very well and the Jones organization, like many other hedge funds, took a serious hit. By year-end 1970, the Securities and Exchange Commission estimated that the fund organization had a mere $30 million under management. It is unclear exactly where the money went, but some was lost to market mistakes and the rest vanished as partners pulled out.

Interestingly enough, the only fund the SEC tracked during that same time period that did not see a decrease in assets was Steinhardt Fine Berkowitz & Co., headed by the soon-to-be-legendary Michael Steinhardt.

By 1977, when the hedge fund industry had plummeted from over $2 billion to roughly $250 million under management, many in the industry thought the concept had seen its day.

Jones himself was quoted in an article in *Institutional Investor* in May 1977 as saying, "I don't believe it [a hedge fund] is ever going to become a big part of the investment scene as it was in the 1960s. . . . The hedge fund does not have a terrific future."[13]

Indeed, as with all things associated with the markets, hedge funds had been going through a rough time; but the cycle soon righted itself. Slowly but surely, through the late 1970s and the 1980s, the industry got back on its feet. It was the bull market of the 1990s, however, that really put hedge funds on the map.

Today the combination of shorting and going long in stocks is second nature to even the most immature Wall Streeter, but 30 years ago it was a daring concept.

Loomis, in her piece "Hard Times Come to the Hedge Funds,"

wrote that her previous story on hedge funds, "The Jones Nobody Keeps Up With," inspired some people to start their own funds, using "the article about Jones as a sort of prospectus, relying on it for help in explaining, and selling, the hedge fund concept to investors."[14]

Slowly but surely, Jones is continuing to get the recognition he deserves. Whether people realize it or not, and most I think do, Alfred Winslow Jones, the sociologist and businessman, created one of Wall Street's most important concepts. His invention gave life to thousands of entrepreneurs and has made and will continue to make many people very wealthy.

How Hedge
Funds Operate

This chapter will explore how hedge funds operate and why blaming them for the ills that rock Wall Street is silly. It is important to understand how to start a hedge fund, who is investing in the vehicles, and who provides services to the industry. It is here that you will read about "the world's greatest investor" and how he came to get this title.

The sport of blaming hedge funds for financial meltdowns was never more apparent than in the summer of 1998 when volatility rocked the world's markets. The near collapse of Long-Term Capital Management LP was splashed across newspapers around the globe, as both a victim and cause of its own demise. Reporters and editors had found a scapegoat for any financial disasters of the 1990s.

It's easy, and it does make a lot of sense, to blame the hedge funds. First, most of them shun publicity and refuse to speak on the record about their strategies or investments. Secondly, many organizations, including the International Monetary Fund (IMF) and the World Bank, not to mention the Securities and Exchange Commission (SEC) and the Federal Reserve System, have trouble tracking hedge fund operators' moves.

So why shouldn't society blame such secretive organizations for its financial woes? When problems strike, why not blame those who are doing well, because surely their success comes at the expense of others?

To understand why blaming hedge funds for every currency crisis and Dow drop is downright silly, we first need to look at who is operating and investing in them. Many of the hedge funds that were once blamed for wreaking havoc on the world's markets were in a state of turmoil as the Asian and Russian crisis of the summer of 1998 took hold. One fund manager believed that Long-Term Capital Management's woes are just the tip of the iceberg and that by year's end more than half of the funds in existence would no longer be around.

"People are not interested in losing money," he said. "The whole reason why investors go with hedge funds is because they want superior returns but also want to be protected when the markets get shaky. Losing half of your assets is not the type of protection that most people have in mind."

This thankfully did not come true. And while many funds did fall, the event of 1998 seemed to be cyclical. The late summer of 1998 displayed a lot of the same characteristics of the 1970s and early 1980s when hedge funds hit hard times. Earlier, the funds had been on a tear, posting very strong returns and attracting many investors and imitators.

For most of the 1950s and 1960s, many people copied and tried to imitate Jones and his staff's method of investing and trading. They wanted to emulate the Jones model, which used a series of long and short positions to put up very significant returns. This strategy worked until the *bear market* started in 1969, when these investment partnerships took it on the chin; most of them eventually went out of business.

The *Fortune* magazine piece titled "Hard Times Come to the Hedge Funds" written by Carol Loomis in January 1970 captures the essence of the hedge fund phenomenon and its explosion. At the time, Loomis estimated that 150 funds around the country had assets under management totaling $1 billion. The hook of the story was that many of the fund managers had not seen 1969's bear market coming. In fact, some funds, including A. W. Jones's, had been negative or flat for the year, causing many of the fund managers to change their strategies and reevaluate their business models. A few went out of business altogether.

bear market   prolonged period of falling prices.

Jones's two partnerships each finished 1969 down over 30 percent for the year, while the New York Stock Exchange composite was off 13 percent.

One of the most interesting points of Loomis's article is revealed in Jones's comments that the problems of 1969 were predicated on Wall Street's "craze for performance" and that "money managers . . . got overconfident about their ability to make money."[1]

One needs only to look at other recent articles in the mainstream press about hedge funds to see that the same sort of euphoria is sweeping the industry today. In the past 10 years, their numbers have exploded. Since 1990, the assets that hedge funds manage have grown tenfold while the number of hedge funds has ballooned at approximately the same rate.

Some people estimate that a new hedge fund opens every day and believe that until the *bull market* bubble bursts and enough people get badly hurt, there will be no end to this trend. One person close to the industry told me that the best thing to happen to hedge funds is that Wall Street is having problems.

bull market   prolonged period of rising prices.

"As long as firms continue to lay off people and pay significantly smaller bonuses, the [hedge fund] industry will continue to be strong," he said. "If you lose your job, what could be easier than setting up a fund? And if you get a small bonus, you think that you can do it yourself and don't need anyone."

As history tells us time and again, the market is about cycles. Hedge funds are not going to be wiped out completely, but it is inevitable that once the bull leaves the ring, a number of them will vanish and the explosive growth in the industry will subside. If some of the biggest, smartest, and most powerful funds took such huge hits from Russia and Asia, prudent thinkers have to believe that others will go down as well.

"It is very simple. A lot of people follow the herd mentality. Right now the herd is going into hedge funds," says one hedge fund manager who requested anonymity. "Eventually, the herd gets wiped out."

STARTING A HEDGE FUND

Today pretty much anyone with a few dollars can start a hedge fund. The most important character traits needed are an ego, an entrepreneurial spirit, and guts. A track record also helps, but in some cases experience is frowned upon—although many observers believe that in light of the carnage of 1998, investors will shy away from fund managers without track records.

A budding manager needs somewhere between $15,000 and $35,000 to cover the costs of the legal work as well as some initial capital. Some managers start with as little investment capital as $25,000, while others jump out of the gate with millions. Once the entity is created and a brokerage account is opened, the manager is in business.

The advances in technology in the past few years have made gathering investment ideas as easy as picking up the phone. Many would-be A. W. Joneses are setting up shop in their living rooms, installing computers and phone lines and placing trades.

One manager told me that it is much more efficient to trade out of his apartment on Manhattan's Upper West Side than from an office downtown. He doesn't have to waste time commuting and he can work no matter what time of day it is without the hassle of riding the subway.

"I no longer need to be on the ground in every country I want to invest in, nor do I have to worry about reporting accounting or broker-age functions because of the strides made in technology in the last few years," says the manager. "Most of the initial information I need is available on the Bloomberg or the Web, and by having a personal com-puter hooked into both, the information is literally a click away. Tech-nology allows me to get the process started a lot quicker and makes the investment process a lot more manageable. It allows me to kick the tires of more companies faster than ever before." "Kicking the tires" is a theme that many of today's up-and-coming managers employ when they go after investment ideas.

It used to be that if you wanted information on companies in Senegal or on stocks in Australia, you needed to be on the ground in the country or wait until your broker opened an office there. Today, the speed at which information travels provides managers access to news and research 24 hours a day, seven days a week. You now can not only get a quote on any stock anywhere in the world but you can also get a map on how to get there by pointing your Web browser to a site and clicking the mouse.

Paul Wong, the fund manager of Edgehill Capital, has constructed what he calls "Hedge Fund Heaven," an office off the entryway of his home in Connecticut where he manages his portfolio and handles all fund operations. In his slice of heaven, Wong has installed a series of ergonomically correct workstations, along with requisite computers, phone lines, and fax machines. He also has a couch and a television with a videocassette recorder.

"Having the office in my home allows me to run a business and be an active father," he says. "I can go to my kids' Little League or tennis matches and then come home and check my positions. I am able to work productively at things that are important to me."

Wong believes the convenience allows him to be not only a better father but a better manager, too. "I can work whenever I want," he says. "I literally can put my kids to bed and be in the office in five minutes looking at reports or scouring the news. I no longer have to carry tons of paper around or spend hours commuting."

Although the community of hedge fund managers and service providers to the industry has been growing quite rapidly in the past few years, it is still relatively small compared to the entire institutional investment community. As such, and as is the case throughout much of Wall Street, many of the industry's players, including the managers, lawyers, and brokers, know each other. Still, as the industry grows many people are not able to keep track of all of the managers and all of the firms doing hedge fund business.

"It used to be that everyone literally knew everyone in this business," says Bill Michaelcheck, president of Mariner Partners, a hedge fund organization profiled in Chapter 3. "Now because everyone and their brother is starting a fund, it is getting harder and harder to know everyone and, more importantly, to know what everyone is doing."

An interesting twist is that many of the marquee names who have been at the forefront of the hedge fund world for decades are slowing down and setting up their children in funds.

Take, for example, Jack Nash, who retired in 1997 from Odyssey Partners and set his son up with a new fund called Ulysses. Michael Steinhardt, who had been threatening to retire for many years, finally did so in 1995, but he has a son who is running his own fund. George Soros's son Robert is active in his father's business, currently managing a piece of Quantum Industrial Holdings and helping to oversee Quantum Realty fund.

According to an article called "The Other Soros" in *Institutional Investor* in March 1998, young Soros says he had no pressure or encouragement from his father to enter the business. Rather, George Soros felt it would be hard for Robert to work in a place where his father cast such a big shadow.

Slowly, the patriarchs of the hedge fund world are passing the torch to the next generation, who no doubt will work very hard to continue the legacy created by their parents.

It was not always as easy to start a hedge fund as it is today. Ten years ago, it would have been hard to find a lawyer or accountant who could help. Of course, many knew of the investment vehicles and understood the structure but there were very few who specialized in the industry. That picture changed with the success of the business and many flocked to it, not only as potential fund managers but as supporting players. This is still true despite the losses of 1998. In fact, many believe that because of the substantial hits many Wall Street firms took, the hedge fund industry will grow at an even faster rate as the millennium draws closer. In plain English, when Wall Street can no longer pay bonuses, people leave and go out on their own.

Today, many of the main figures in the hedge fund industry work together, and through a network of referrals you can find some of the best legal and financial talent available. It takes just one phone call to schedule an appointment with an accountant, a lawyer, and a prime broker.

"The idea is to provide as much service as we can to the manager in order to make sure we are able to get and hold on to the business," explains an employee at one of the leading prime brokerage firms. "Although hedge funds are a dime a dozen, the key is to work with funds that are going to grow and be successful so that over time the business grows from within instead of relying constantly on new clients."

Many of the service providers, attracted by the industry's exponential growth, market their organizations as one-stop shopping sources for all the fund managers' needs. At conferences and seminars, prime brokers team up with lawyers who are connected to accountants who work with third-party marketing agents, all in the name of service and, of course, the generation of fees.

Experts ascribe the growth of hedge funds to the acceptance by the investing public of alternative investments and to the fact that people in general have more dollars to invest.

"There are many people who have a lot more money today than a few years ago, and they are looking for better returns than they can get in mutual funds or individual stocks," says a fund manager who recently retired and requested anonymity. "The strength of the economy has not hurt the industry. When people make millions of dollars through stock options and initial public offerings, eventually they realize they have to do something with the money if they want to hold on to it.

"Sure, they can put it in mutual funds or individual stocks, but they would rather put it into something exotic that may pay better returns and give them something to talk about at cocktail parties," he continues.

As the market grows, people are looking for investment opportunities that are unique and that will provide them with greater returns. The ability of a hedge fund to use any means necessary to post increased returns makes it very attractive both to investors and to potential managers.

Over the past few years, a number of independent studies have shown that, on average, hedge funds post higher rates of return than those of the S&P 500 and other benchmarks. This ability continually to outperform the market appeals to potential individual investors who are looking for higher returns and are not concerned necessarily with the accompanying higher risk.

Still, there are naysayers who believe hedge funds' ability to outperform the market is overstated.

One of them is George Van, chairman of Van Hedge Fund Advisors, a consultant to potential hedge fund investors, who believes that in some cases the return isn't worth the risk, that many funds barely beat the S&P year after year while taking substantial chances with investors' money. Van believes the key to investing in hedge funds is to find the right fund and, more importantly, the right manager.

His company produced Figure 2.1, which illustrates how various strategies have performed since 1988. On a net compounded annual return, Van's Hedge Fund Index was up 17.8 percent for the five-year period while the S&P 500 was up 20.3 percent and the average stock mutual fund was up 14.9 percent. Recall that in general a mutual fund does not take as many risks as a hedge fund, nor does it have the same high fee structure. Mutual funds are also bound by significant amounts of regulation and oversight by the Securities and Exchange Commission.

Veterans of the industry often question the excitement surrounding hedge funds and point to the fact that many of today's managers

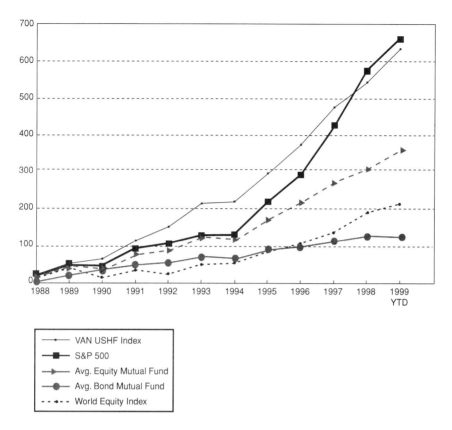

FIGURE 2.1 Cumulative Returns of Hedge Funds vs. Major Market Indices 1988 Through Second Quarter 1999.
Copyright 1999 Van Hedge Fund Advisors, Inc.

have never seen a down market. These old-timers question the new-comers' ability to handle the market when it corrects itself. As the market nose-dived in the summer of 1998, it was becoming more and more apparent that these sentiments rang true.

"It is too easy for people to get into the industry," says Jim Rogers, president of Rogers Holdings and a former partner of George Soros. "When we started out, it was a lot harder and there was nobody around to help us. Now there are brokerage firms, law firms, and accounting firms all specializing in hedge funds, which makes getting into the business easy."

Michael Steinhardt, who had more than 30 years of stellar performance, disagrees with Rogers in that he believes hedge funds *always* have been an easy business to get into. "How many other businesses are there where with just a few years of experience you can hang out your shingle in a relatively unregulated industry and get 20 percent of the upside on other people's money?" he asks. "Ease of entry into the business is extraordinary. It always was but it was a psychic leap for people in the sixties and seventies to invest in hedge funds. Today, everybody wants to run a hedge fund and everybody else thinks they should be investing in one."

What has lowered the barrier in the past 10 years is Wall Street's understanding of how profitable providing services to the hedge fund community can be. The issue now is what happens to the industry when the market cracks.

"Starting a hedge fund is probably the most efficient way to make money in the financial world today," Rogers says. "The problem is once things start to turn, people will lose money and things will get ugly, and when they get ugly everyone loses."

Today, more than a dozen organizations will assist potential fund managers in drafting legal documents, provide brokerage services, and also help with marketing and money raising.

What makes the whole industry so incestuous is that even when people blow up or self-destruct, they can still find work in it and often are able to profit handsomely from their mistakes. More likely than not they will come back either as money managers or in the form of other cogs on the gears that make the industry spin.

When Victor Niederhoffer's operation blew up in October 1997, people said he would never manage money again. The evening after the morning he was shut down, I was at an industry function talking to one of his investors who, prior to the collapse, had been one of his staunchest supporters. The investor told me that he had never seen anything so ugly, and not everything had been fully disclosed.

"This mess is so big, I don't think he will ever be able to work in this industry again," the investor said. "Nothing can save him."

However, saved he was. Four months later the following ad ran in *The Wall Street Journal's* help wanted section:

FINANCIAL MARKETS

Wanted: Individual with good quantitative mind, creativity, programming skills and interested in aspects of financial markets to work in a small, innovative, formerly successful trading firm in CT. Must be flexible and willing to learn. Low starting salary, excellent potential. Fax resume to Victor Niederhoffer . . . .[2]

The man who prides himself on reading no newspaper other than the *National Enquirer* was back. But, how? How was it possible to have lost so much and yet come back so quickly? The answer is one part ego, one part stamina, and one part rich friends.

Niederhoffer had proved himself a solid money manager. Like a number of people in the industry today, he insisted on making his story known; he wrote a book, gave many interviews, and was available to anyone who would listen to his story. He was known as someone who could bet heavily on one side of the market only to be wrong and then miraculously recover—a wild trader who performed well in any market condition. He also had some very wealthy friends, or, more accurately, one very wealthy friend: George Soros. It seems that unlike most other areas of Wall Street where you are only as good as your last trade, with Niederhoffer it did not matter. Through his connections he was able to reestablish himself and begin trading again. Niederhoffer would not comment on where the money for his current fund came from, but many in the hedge fund world believe a good portion of it came from Soros.[3]

Another money manager who blew up in December 1997 after losing almost all of her partners' capital by betting on micro-cap stocks has found a niche for herself on the marketing side of the business. After a bit of time spent soul-searching, she set up a firm in midtown Manhattan that specializes in third-party marketing of hedge funds, which means she is helping them to attract investment capital. She works within a network of wealthy individuals, family offices (limited partnerships or limited liability companies), and institutions, helping them decide where to put their money.

"Most hedge fund managers I have met and worked with have two problems when it comes to raising money: Number one, they have no interest in marketing, and two, they don't know how to do it," she says. "My experience in both raising money for my own fund as well as having worked in institutional sales has allowed me to build a network of potential investors that are interested in finding a good manager who has a good strategy and who will provide them with solid returns. I believe that I bring strength to both sides of the equation—I know how to pick good managers and I know how to find money."

Both of these cases illustrate that there is life after death in the hedge fund industry. The Long-Term Capital case presented earlier proves that if you know the right people, you may not have to find work after you blow up.

Before you can blow up, however, you need to create an organization. There are four essential puzzle pieces: money, a lawyer, an accountant, and a prime broker.

Once you find a lawyer, the next item on the list is usually a prime broker, who serves as office manager, back-office support person, and something like an execution clerk. Prime brokers provide almost everything a fund manager needs to get started. Accountants are least important at start-up but most important after the first year, when the accountant brings validity to the track record, one of the most important tools in helping to raise money. And an accountant makes it all official.

As for money, it takes surprisingly little. Most fund managers start out with having enough money in the bank to cover living expenses for a year or two, plus what they have invested in the fund and some for administrative expenses, so that they do not have to worry about where money is coming from to pay bills and live while they are building their business.

One fund manager told me that she waited for almost two years before she launched her fund to make sure she had enough to cover living expenses for at least two years. "I knew it would be a very long time before I would be able to take out any of the money I earned in the fund and live on it, so I knew I had to have a lot of money in the bank to ensure it was not a problem."

She also wanted to make sure that she didn't need any money she did earn from the fund, so that she could invest it right back into the fund and continue to increase her stake.

Some of the most significant costs of doing business are those associated with administering the fund. Administration costs range from data feeds and execution costs to rent and telephone bills. Many new fund managers try to keep these expenses down by working with a prime broker that will provide all the services as part of a package. Once the fund is up and running, though, many managers build elaborate office complexes and install large organizations to run and administer the operation. This is in direct contrast to A. W. Jones, who was often ridiculed by his partners and employees for not wanting to spend money on a large office filled with modern accoutrements.

Prime brokers provide the up-and-coming as well as the established hedge fund manager with everything from execution services and daily profit-and-loss statements to Bloomberg terminals and office space.

Some of today's leading prime brokers are Morgan Stanley Dean Witter & Co., Furman Selz, Goldman Sachs Group LP, Bear, Stearns & Co. Inc., and NationsBanc Montgomery Securities. Since operating a hedge fund is very lucrative to the fund's manager, being the prime broker to a successful fund can be very lucrative to the Wall Street firm providing the services.

In an article in the summer 1998 issue of *Global Custodian*, a trade magazine published in Greenwich, Connecticut, George Palmer wrote that when he was interviewing an executive in the equities department of Goldman Sachs in 1990, the person told him, "You should meet our prime brokerage people, they are our diamond in the rough." The only thing that has changed since is that many more firms have realized that prime brokerage is a diamond in the rough and as such have started to offer the services.

The idea is very simple. The brokerage firm provides the hedge fund manager with custody and clearing. As perks, if you will, firms also provide managers with office space, data feeds, phone lines, and everything else they need to run their business. Besides paying a fee for the services, the fund manager and the prime broker have an understanding: The manager will route some of his or her trades through the prime broker's trading desks—which in turn will generate commissions. There is no written agreement that says this nor is there a requirement as to how many trades must be sent to the brokerage firm. That would be illegal. There is, however, an unwritten rule and managers know that if the prime broker does not see some commission dollars, they will be asked to take their business elsewhere.

"For the most part, we get a good share of our customers' business," says Stephan Vermut, president and chief executive of NationsBanc Montgomery Securities Prime Brokerage Unit. "We do not force people to trade with us, nor do we expect to see them send every trade through to our desks. We do however expect some orders from the managers."

Vermut says his company usually receives 20 to 30 percent of its clients' commission dollars, which he says is the industry norm. Other prime brokers agreed, saying that if a customer does not send at least 20 percent of its trades to the prime broker's order desks, the manager will be asked to look elsewhere for a prime broker.

"Some people do all of their business through us while others do just a fraction," Vermut says. "In the end, the numbers make sense and the business model has worked very well for us."

Remember, it is very easy for the prime broker to keep track of the fund's trades and where it executes the orders because the firm keeps its books and records. On any given day at any given hour the firm acting as a prime broker can look at screens and see which funds are trading with it and which are trading away and immediately determine which relationships make sense.

Although the field of firms providing prime brokerage service is quite crowded, there are a few that stand out. Morgan Stanley Dean Witter is by far the biggest provider in terms of assets under management of prime brokerage services, but it seems that Furman Selz is by far the most popular because it is willing to work funds of any size and experience. NationsBanc Montgomery Securities seems to be the fastest growing firm that provides prime brokerage services and through its use of technology—in particular its World Wide Web trade reporting product—many fund managers believe it is the most sophisticated service provider.

In its annual survey of the industry, *Global Custodian* found that some other companies have started to capture market share, including Merrill Lynch & Co. Inc., PaineWebber Group Inc., Lehman Brothers Holdings Inc., and Daiwa Securities. The survey observed that "prime brokerage is one of the few operationally intensive businesses where brokerage houses are better positioned than banks however that is not stopping banks from stepping up their efforts to service hedge funds."[4]

"It used to be that when you signed on a new client, you broke open a bottle of champagne," says one person who has been in the prime brokerage business since the mid-1980s. "After the crash, the business took off and has never been the same since. Now we can add one or two new clients a month." Instead of bubbles flowing at prime brokers, the money is.

The reason the hedge fund business exploded in the late 1980s was that many on Wall Street realized that their careers and, more important, their bonuses were tied to others. They came to believe it was not worth the risk of losing their jobs because someone else made a mistake.

"By opening up hedge funds they could be their own boss and know that they did not have to worry about how others performed," says one observer. "They just had to rely on themselves."

Today the prime brokerage business represents a significant piece of revenue for many firms. Goldman Sachs, for instance, which for years said it would not work with managers who were just starting or who managed only a small amount of assets, has changed that policy and will now work with almost anyone. The reason? Nobody knows where the next Soros, Robertson, or Steinhardt will come from. And the firm does not want to miss out on potentially huge sources of revenue that may come down the road.

In the past few years, NationsBanc Montgomery Securities has

built its prime brokerage business to the point that many in the industry believe it to be the best because it is so technologically advanced. The entire franchise is based on technology, especially its
back-office systems. It's designed to put all reporting and analytical
functions at a manager's fingertips via the Internet. Not only does the
system store current data, but it also provides historical information.
The system is designed so that a manager does not have to wait for reports to be delivered or to have documents retrieved to get a picture
of the fund's situation.

"When we came to Montgomery, we knew that we needed to
come up with a way to differentiate ourselves from the pack," says Vermut. "We realized that the way to do it was with technology. We created a system that puts all of the functionality that a hedge fund
manager was accustomed to getting on paper onto the Internet."

Vermut and his colleagues' bet has proved successful. In the four
years the firm has been in business it has grown to more than 300
clients with over $2 billion in assets.

For a number of years, Furman Selz was one of the few games in
town. It was where most people turned for help in setting up and operating a hedge fund.

"Many people went to Furman Selz because they would take you
if you were small and believed that you would make it," says someone
who works in prime brokerage but wants to remain anonymous.
"Now firms like Goldman Sachs have decided that size does not matter, and they have realized that if they take on a firm with five or ten
million dollars and the fund manager is successful, they will have the
fund for life and, more important, a steady stream of continuously
growing revenue."

Because prime brokers operate in obscurity like their clients,
the industry is very small. There is a certain unwritten rule not to
poach clients while so many people are starting funds. "We would
never go after a client of another firm and for the most part no one
will," says a prime broker. "But as soon as the market turns and the
explosion in fund creation ends, it will be open season and no one's
clients will be safe."

The nature of the business is such that it is a cash cow.

"Our business is a safe bread-and-butter business that allows the firm to profit handsomely for providing services while taking very little risk," asserts a person in the prime brokerage industry. "We have never had a situation evolve where we lost money or took a capital hit when a fund blew up. The most we can ever lose is commission dollars. If a fund blows up, we will replace it with another."

Just to be on the safe side, in light of the blow-up of Long-Term Capital and the refusal of Bear, Stearns, to participate in the bailout because it believed it had too much at stake being the fund's clearing agent, many firms reevaluated their risk exposure to make sure a fund blow-up would not do the firm in with it. According to one prime broker, management at his firm did not really understand what function it provided funds and as such got very seared when they read about Long-Term Capital.

"I was called a number of times by people on the management committee requesting information about what sort of losses we should expect to sustain in light of all the funds losing money," he says. "When I told them none, they were shocked and quite relieved."

Most prime brokerages have office suites throughout Manhattan and other key cities that they lease to hedge fund managers. In some areas of midtown Manhattan, if you throw a rock through a window you are likely to hit a hedge fund more often than not. The same can be said of San Francisco, Dallas, and Boston. Prime brokers also operate offices for fund managers in London, Tokyo, Zurich, and Paris.

The offices around 44th Street and Park Avenue in midtown Manhattan, often called Hedge Fund Row or the Hedge Fund Hotel, are quite interesting to visit. Aside from sharing a common reception area and series of conference rooms, each office is its own little world of high finance. In one room you may have a fund that specializes in special situation equity plays, in another you may find a manager who trades foreign currency options, while a third may simply trade small-cap equities that are linked to the financial services industry. Each has a different strategy and management style, yet some may have the same investors.

Prime brokerage services are just a small part of what is often thought of as a sophisticated world of hedge fund operations. In reality, like most businesses, the fundamentals of operating a hedge fund are quite simple.

In most cases there are just three aspects to the business: marketing and raising capital, legal and accounting work, and investing and trading. Most managers do not want to have anything to do with the first two and therefore farm them out to third parties. In the past few years, managers have found they can pretty much get all of their trades executed and their legal work and accounting functions handled by outsourcing at a fraction of what it would cost to do them in-house.

"Most hedge fund managers have no interest in marketing and, more important, don't have any idea as to how to do it," says Barbara Doran, managing director of Global Capital Strategies LLC in New York, a third-party marketing firm.

When Doran works with a fund, her job is to find investors. She promotes the fund and its manager to everyone from wealthy individuals and family offices to corporations and endowments. Doran, like other third-party marketers, is paid a fee for bringing in capital. In most cases the marketing firm works on an exclusive basis just as a real estate broker would if you were trying to sell your home.

In today's competitive marketplace the key to survival is the ability to attract and keep investors. To do so, a manager must put up solid returns quarter after quarter and the marketer must be able to tell likely investors a compelling story.

Many managers run into a catch-22 when it comes to attracting new investors. In most cases new managers have very little track record of their own and therefore they do not have much muscle behind their story. While traders may have been successful at Goldman or Salomon and received huge bonuses, who is to say what they will do on their own or how much of their success was based on their own effort? Therefore, managers who strike out on their own need to have a large group of contacts and character witnesses who can bring potential investors to the table.

A recent trend in the industry is that of large, established hedge funds and money management firms placing investment dollars with start-ups.

One fund manager that I spoke with had been approached by a number of the hedge fund world's marquee names offering to invest in the new fund. At first the manager could not believe the good fortune. But this situation had a number of strings attached. When the manager sat down with the potential investors' representatives, it turned out the hedge funds wanted to wield a lot of control over investment decisions and wanted to split all of the new fund's fees.[5] The manager decided that although it would be great to have their money in the fund, it would be better in the long run to do without it.

"They wanted too much control and I did not think it would be worth it," the manager explains. "In the short run it would have been nice to have their money, but over time it would have been a problem. It was very difficult to walk away from their money, but looking back I am glad I did."

According to a person close to a large hedge fund, the reason many funds like to farm money out is because it usually offers a win-win situation for both parties.

"The new fund managers get a good chunk of money which allows them to get established while we usually get the best years of their performance," he says.

The reason many large hedge funds are looking for smaller funds to put their money with is slippage, a fund manager's ability to get in and out of investments with large sums of money without causing the market to move.

It is very hard to move large sums of money in and out of good investments. A manager who likes a stock that is thinly traded needs to be careful that going in or out does not cause the market for the stock to move significantly. Often even the rumor of a hedge fund's going into a stock can cause market turmoil. So a big fund becomes limited as to what it can and cannot buy. It is a lot easier to find places to invest smaller amounts of money, so by putting money with a new fund, a large fund is able to capitalize on situations that otherwise would not be available.

For the most part, once a manager takes money from another manager, there is a confidentiality agreement that does not let the manager who is receiving the money speak about the fund that is providing it. Of course, as long as it does not appear in print, most managers are willing to give up the name to potential investors because it is a pat on the back. If George Soros or Julian Robertson likes this guy and has given him money, why shouldn't you?[6]

"Many large hedge funds spread the dollars around in order to continually put up strong numbers, and in most cases it is good for young managers who can get these investments. The problem is they can't tell anyone about it," says an industry observer who requested anonymity. "If the world knew that some of the largest funds were doling out money to people who were still wet behind the ears, how do you think that they would react when the performance comes in and they have to pay such a large percent of the profits to people who did not even do any work?"

Regardless of the outside investors, the most important aspect of a start-up fund is the manager's own stake. Even established funds would have a hard time raising money if the manager did not have a significant stake in the fund. Investors are saying to the managers: "Put your money where your mouth is."

Unlike most mutual funds, which bar managers from investing in the funds they manage, a hedge fund is doomed if managers do not have their own money in it. It really does not matter how much, but some managers put every penny they have in their fund.

One manager told me that at one point he was putting so much into his fund that the gas and electric company was threatening to cut off service to his home. His office assistant finally persuaded him to take some money out of the fund to live on, but he says it was difficult because he believed so strongly in what he was doing that he wanted to have as much invested as possible.

As hedge funds continue to become more popular, many future Wall Streeters are going right into business for themselves instead of working for a brokerage firm or hedge fund. A number of funds have been started recently by people in their early twenties who have had some luck in the market, using $50,000 to $100,000 of family money.

One fund manager started his fund while in high school and ran it through four years of college. In the spring of 1998, he told his investors that he would be closing the fund and would liquidate all of its positions by year-end. He wrote in his annual letter to investors: "After serious thought, I have reached the inescapable conclusion that I will not be able to work for somebody else and simultaneously manage [the fund]. After graduation I must just join the real world and find gainful employment."

I wonder if the manager's investors knew he was not in "the real world" while he was investing their "real money" in "real securities," and although he had "real gains" he could instead have had "real losses."

Most hedge fund managers understand that they operate in a "real world" and that their "real careers" are on the line based on their investment decisions. This is not always the case with those who cover the industry. The popular press is often quick to criticize managers because they are apt to make a deal when it comes to accepting new investors.

Nobody is forced to invest with a manager. An individual or institution does it by choice. In all cases it is up to the investor to perform due diligence and determine if the manager's investment ideas and criteria mesh with their own investment objectives.

An article in *Forbes* in April 1998 questioned one manager in particular because the minimum investment in his fund was "negotiable" and because he ran the fund out of his apartment in Manhattan.[7]

The same article also questioned famed hedge fund operator Julian Robertson for having lowered his minimum investment to $1 million from $10 million and for requiring new investors to sign an agreement not to withdraw their money "for five years, even if Robertson 'goes insane, dies or becomes incapacitated.' " The story did not mention, however, his stellar track record for the previous 20-odd years or his continuing ability to reinvent his investment strategies. That's what allows him to take advantage of the world's ever-changing economic landscape.

HEDGE FUND REGULATIONS AND STRUCTURES

When Loomis wrote her *Fortune* article, she looked at some of the people who were investing in hedge funds. As can be expected, a list of names was very hard to come by, but she found a who's who of the nation's rich and famous. It includes Laurence Tisch, Daniel Searle, Keith Funston, Deborah Kerr, Jimmy Stewart, Jack Palance, and Rod Steiger. Today the lists of investors (which are even harder to come by) also read like a who's who of the nation's rich and famous.

One hedge fund investor who should be noted is Laurence Tisch. A very savvy businessman, he has had not such good luck with picking hedge fund managers. Although he refuses to comment on whether he still invests in hedge funds, it is widely known that he is an investor in John Meriwether's Long-Term Capital through a company he owns. It is believed that when he heard of the firm's losses, he immediately asked for a redemption and wanted to get what little money he had left out.

Neither Meriwether nor Tisch would confirm this story, nor would Tisch comment on his investment practices. An article in *The Wall Street Journal* revealed that Tisch did have some money invested in Long-Term Capital through Loews Corp. The article says that the Tisch exposure to Long-Term Capital was a result of its purchase of Continental Insurance of New York in 1995. The insurance company had invested $10 million in Long-Term Capital in 1994 and it received a payout in December 1997 of approximately $18.25 million. The company kept $10 million in the fund and saw that get marked down to under $1 million when Long-Term Capital collapsed.[8]

It also widely known that Tisch did have substantial positions in a number of hedge funds in the 1960s and 1970s that went belly-up. At the time, he was quoted as saying he'd had it with the hedge funds.

In early 1998, KPMG Peat Marwick released a study titled "The

Coming Evolution of the Hedge Fund Industry: A Case for Growth and Restructuring," which says affluent private investors represent more than 80 percent of the hedge fund assets, and the remaining 20 percent consists of institutional investors, including college endowments, pension funds, foundations, and insurance companies.

My own alma mater, Clark University, is an active investor in hedge funds. According to James Collins, the university's executive vice president for administration and finance, Clark has been investing in hedge funds since 1993. "The university's investment committee decided to invest in hedge funds because we wanted to diversify our risk exposure and work with some of the smartest minds on Wall Street."

Clark has approximately 20 percent of its endowment invested in five hedge funds, all of which use different investment strategies. To find the fund managers, the university relied on a number of existing relationships its board of trustees had with Wall Street. Members of the investment committee as well as university officials meet and talk with the fund managers on a regular basis to keep tabs on the investments.

"The program is working as we thought it would, and we expect to continue seeing absolute returns of 10 percent to 11 percent from the investments," Collins says. "Over time we believe it will prove to be the right investment for the university's money."

The KPMG study found that as the economy continued to get stronger, many more people are becoming eligible to invest in hedge funds. The company expects assets that are available for investment to grow from $10 trillion in 1996 to over $16 trillion by 2001. The growth rate for hedge funds is similarly strong. KPMG expects the industry to grow at an annual rate of 26 percent a year to over $500 billion in assets by 2001 and to increase tenfold to over $1.7 trillion in 10 years.[9]

Investor money comes from all sorts of sources today: college endowments, state pension funds, municipalities, corporations, family offices, and, of course, the wealthy.

As recently as 1990, many corporations and other institutional investors shied away from hedge funds, but this situation has changed as more and more people learn of the types of returns they can get.

"Hedge fund investors are no longer an elite core of the world's wealthiest investors," says Steinhardt. "Publicity about sustained superior returns attracted hordes of money into funds. But many of the old funds such as mine had high minimums and were closed to new money. That alone created a certain mystique about hedge fund investing."

Now, however, because of the proliferation of information as well as market forces, hedge fund data and resources are readily available through sources ranging from specialized consulting firms to web sites. If you type the phrase "hedge fund" into a search engine on the Internet, it will come up with hundreds, if not thousands, of sites that offer some sort of information on the subject.

Another factor that is causing hedge fund information to be more readily available is the change in the regulations surrounding the number of investors.

In 1996, the National Securities Markets Improvement Act quintupled the number of investors allowed in hedge funds to 500. Since hedge funds began in the late 1940s, the total number of investors allowed had been 100. Sometimes fund managers and their lawyers interpreted the law so they could have only 99 investors because they also counted the general partner as a limited partner. However, according to Richard Valentine, a former partner at the law firm of Seward & Kissel, the general partner did not need to be counted.

"People thought that they had to count the general partner as an investor and therefore could only have 99 other slots, but in reality, if they wrote the partnership agreements properly, the general partner did not have to count," he says.

Although the law is pretty clear on limits placed on advertising and marketing—they are not allowed—many fund managers realize that to reap the benefits of the new legislation they need to get their message out. Therefore it is not uncommon today to find an article in the major financial press that touches on hedge funds or focuses on various aspects of the industry. In light of the losses of 1998, this statement has never been more true about the industry. Many managers want to distance themselves from the others and are therefore willing to state their case now more than ever.

A lot of fund managers have also started to become more interested about the world's markets and national economic policies. The Securities and Exchange Commission still does not let hedge fund managers use conventional methods of advertising. Some say this has helped create the mystique of the industry and its managers, while others believe it ensures the safety of unsuspecting investors.

"By not letting fund managers advertise or market their businesses, the SEC has created a veil of secrecy over the industry that really helps the managers attract business," says an industry observer. "People in general are more interested in things that they are told they cannot learn about or do not have easy access to, and therefore it has become easier in some cases for managers to attract investors. People want what others cannot have."

Most of the prime brokers work with their fund managers to help them raise capital. But because the funds are not allowed to advertise, this process can be quite difficult. Often a brokerage firm will put together a report on a number of fund managers, detailing their strategies and performances but without actually naming the specifics. Once investors have the opportunity to review the information, they contact the firm and the firm will alert the manager. The manager will then contact the potential investor. Before any meeting, the manager most likely will put the investor through a suitability test to ensure that they are not wasting time by talking to unqualified investors.

"The process is hard, but it is the only way we have been able to figure out to market the funds without running the risk of running afoul of the law," says a person who markets hedge funds for a prime broker.

The change in the regulations allows funds to expand the number of limited partners they can have and redefines the guidelines under which an investor must qualify to invest.

Prior to the change, the only requirement was to be an *accredited investor,* which is defined as someone who has $1 million net worth, including a primary residence, or an annual salary for two consecutive years of $200,000 ($300,000 for a couple) that is expected to continue. While there are set rules as to who can invest in a hedge fund there are no such rules when it comes to minimum investments. Investments can range from as little as $50,000 to as much as $100 million; it all depends on the size of the fund. Now that the regulations have changed to allow for more investors, some believe that minimums will come down.

accredited investor   an investor who meets the Securities and Exchange Commission guidelines required for investing in hedge funds.

The current regulation now allows for 500 limited partners as long as the fund or entity has not accepted any investors who do not meet the qualified purchaser requirements after September 1996. The fund manager has to make it clear in the offering documents that future investors will be limited to qualified purchasers and has to make available to all pre-September 1996 investors the ability to withdraw their investments at net asset value without penalty.

According Jonathan Baum, a lawyer who specializes in securities law, a qualified purchaser is defined as any trust, natural person, or family-controlled company that owns not less than $5 million in investments, and any person, acting for his or her own account or that of other qualified purchasers, who owns and invests on a discretionary basis not less than $25 million.

"The change in the regulation has been a great thing for large funds like Tiger that can attract the really high-net-worth individuals and institutions, but for the little guys who can't fill their first one hundred slots, there is no need for this yet," says Peter Testaverde, a partner in Goldstein Golub Kessler, an accounting firm in New York that has a significant hedge fund business. "This whole thing is about the [Securities and Exchange] Commission understanding that people with a net worth of a billion dollars do not need the same protection as Joe Retail when it comes to investing."

Hedge funds for the most part operate as limited partnerships and in some cases as limited liability companies. They are registered as either *onshore funds* or *offshore funds,* allowing for different groups of investors.

onshore fund   an investment vehicle that is set up in the United States that is available to U.S. citizens.

Today lawyers use boilerplate language for hedge funds' investment memorandums, spelling out to potential investors the structure and strategy of the entity and describing its fund manager. A potential investor needs to realize that the memorandum is designed to protect the fund manager, so it is very important that potential investors perform their own independent due diligence before investing. Reading the investment memorandum is just a beginning.

offshore fund   an investment vehicle that is set up outside of the United States and is managed from a low tax jurisdiction that is not available to U.S. citizens.

Still, there are a number of things that are important to look at when reading an investment memo, including lockup provisions, fee structures, and the type of investments the fund manager plans to make. In most cases, the funds lock up money for one to three years and then allow for withdrawals quarterly. When it comes to explaining what the fund plans to buy and sell, the memos are usually very vague. They say things like, "The manager may use his or her discretion to invest in any or all of the following at any given point in time."

The memo will most likely list every single type of security, commodity, or futures contract known to the markets. This is done to provide the manager with latitude. In most cases, though, managers tend to stick to one or two types of securities or commodities, and that information is usually findable in other areas of the investment memo. The reason for the vague language is freedom. Managers need to have flexibility to invest.

Overall, the best advice for a potential investor is to get help when picking a manager the first or second time. Often that advice comes from other investors. One manager told me that he has a husband-and-wife team that comes off as mild and somewhat naive until they start asking questions about the fund and its investment and management style.

"These sweet old nice people become Attila the Hun as soon as we start talking about money and investment strategy," he says. "A lot of managers think investors are not so smart or with-it, and it is a mistake. If they weren't so smart or with-it, they wouldn't be qualified to invest in hedge funds."

There are many different groups of investors in hedge funds today than when Jones started out. Some call these investors greedy, but most of Wall Street believes its best and brightest minds are working for hedge funds. If you truly want to beat the market as well as take advantage of various investment styles that are not open to the general public, hedge funds are the only place to put your money, assuming you meet the investment qualifications.

In most cases, there is plenty of information about funds made available by the fund operators and their marketing agents. In addition, a number of analytical organizations track the industry. Many funds have web sites, and managers are often quoted in newspaper and magazine stories. The explosion in hedge funds has also been greeted by an explosion in hedge fund consulting firms. These so-called independent agencies offer potential investors insight into various styles and strategies. The services also provide data and other relevant information on thousands of funds.

In light of the carnage of 1998, there have been some questions and a few small scandals regarding the independence of a number of funds. Some independent advisers have been accused of not telling potential investors that they have an arrangement with a hedge fund they recommended and that they receive a fee from it for bringing in new investors. It is not the point of this book to say that these advisers are unethical, but the publisher and the author believe it is our duty to warn the reader of unethical practices by some firms.

The best bet in finding a hedge fund is to use someone you know and trust as an adviser. It is up to investors to understand the type of investment they are getting into, and the only way to do that is to get involved personally.

One aspect of hedge funds that is often confusing is the use of offshore and onshore investment vehicles by fund managers. Many managers have both an onshore fund and an offshore fund, which operate with something called a "master feeder" fund. This structure allows the manager to pool all of the funds' assets in one vehicle that splits gains and losses based on the assets of its onshore and offshore partners.

If, for example, the onshore fund has $60 million and the offshore fund has $40 million, 60 percent of the profits and losses would go to the onshore fund and 40 percent would go to the offshore fund.

"Using this structure allows the fund manager to make sure everybody gets the same rate of return and they don't have to worry about entering an order and allocating the proceeds," says Testaverde. "It is a cleaner way of doing things and gives everybody the same results."

Many fund managers use offshore funds—which are defined as entities that are not registered in the United States because they want to preserve the anonymity of their investors and to avoid a number of tax issues associated with having a fund registered in the United States. "Going offshore ensures complete investor confidentiality but it also means that the fund cannot accept American investors," says securities law expert Jonathan Baum.

The regulations surrounding hedge funds for the most part end with the number of investors and with the definition of who can invest in the funds.

It is hard to define exactly what a hedge fund is because the various structures used around the globe by managers are so diverse. The clearest definition comes from *Merriam Webster's Collegiate Dictionary,* which defines the investment vehicle as "an investing group usually in the form of a limited partnership that employs speculative techniques in the hope of obtaining large capital gains."

One very famous fund manager told me that the only definition of a hedge fund that he had ever read that made sense to him was the one by Carol Loomis published in *Fortune* magazine 30 years ago: "A hedge fund is a limited partnership organized to invest in securities, with a partnership structured in such a way as to give the general partners— the managers of the fund—a share of the profits earned on the money."[10]

Loomis went to great lengths to ensure that the reader could differentiate between a hedge fund and a simple limited partnership that makes investments:

> The structure has three main features: first, the partnership arrangement, through which managers of a fund can be compensated in such a way as to leave them highly motivated to do well; second, the use of borrowed money to obtain leverage, [a] technique permitting the fund to take maximum advantage of a bull market; and third, the use of short selling as a hedge, or protection against the bear market.[11]

What is interesting is that many within the industry as well as those covering it define the hedge fund by its investment guidelines as set forth by the Securities and Exchange Commission. Rather than understanding how the vehicle operates, many reporters and industry observers choose to define the vehicles by who can invest, not by what they do.

When I met with Loomis in the spring of 1998, we discussed her articles and the lasting effects they seem to have on the industry. She says she finds it surprising that in all this time, people still turned to these pieces for information and ideas on how the industry operates and how to get started in it.

According to one industry observer, everybody in New York except the cabdrivers is starting a hedge fund for one simple reason: *money.*

"You are seeing a lot of investment professionals leaving their firms and starting funds because they think that they can make more money by not having to share the P&L [profit and loss] with upper management," he points out. "A lot of research guys and traders are also jumping in because it is a phenomenon that is going to work in good times and bad.

"Many people are looking to invest in hedge funds because they are greedy and want to outperform the market," he continues. "If people were satisfied with the returns of the S&P or the Dow, not only would there not be so many hedge funds but there would be a lot less business on Wall Street."

He believes that the reason hedge funds will grow in bad times as well as good is the egos that put people on Wall Street to begin with: "In good times, people don't want to share profits with the house and they believe they can do it on their own; in bad times a lot of talented people lose their jobs and they have egos large enough to let them go out on their own."

That was until the shake-up of the summer of 1998. Now some people are more cautious. One of the greatest advantages to hedge funds had been the manager's ability to use any means necessary to find profitable places to put money. Now that a number of the most exciting places have once again fallen on hard times and many hedge funds have lost large amounts of money, the number of people who want to exploit these exotic opportunities may be getting smaller.

When a fund goes from having $300 million under management on Friday to having just under $200 million in assets on Tuesday, it's hard to attract new money.

HOW HEDGE FUNDS USE LEVERAGE

One of the industry's problems is that a lot of managers who find themselves in trouble are not using the Jones model and thus are not running true hedge funds. Most funds today do not hedge as Jones did throughout his career but rather use large amounts of leverage, which allows them to capture enormous gains on even the smallest price movements. Although Jones was a great believer in leverage, he also believed in executing short positions in order to have a cushion in case the market fell out from under him. Many managers only use short positions sporadically and therefore are not protected when things do not go their way. To be protected, a hedge fund needs to have a significant amount of short positions.

Leverage, despite what much of the press thinks, is not a dirty word. Often those who employ a Jones model will use a 70 percent to 40 percent split of long to short positions. Leverage is an important tool that when used properly can boost returns while limiting risk.

A very simple example is the following situation: If a fund is 75 percent long and 25 percent short, the fund is net long 50 percent—a bullish posture in which the shorts have to work three times as hard as the longs. However, through the use of leverage, the same fund could be 125 percent long and 75 percent short, giving the fund, while it is still net long 50 percent, greater protection on the downside. In this example, the shorts only have to work 1.7 times as hard as the longs. This is business school Leverage 101, and it is something not to be feared but to be embraced by both fund managers and investors.

Prior to the summer of 1998, the hedge fund world had been for the most part flying below the radar screens of the world beyond Wall Street. The one aspect that did become quite newsworthy was that a number of the industry's most famous managers had decided to return capital to investors.

These so-called Midas traders have amassed a fortune for both themselves and their partners by doing what they do best: investing money and picking winners. They have also become more realistic in the past few years. There have been many instances where these Midas traders have had to return capital to investors because it was time for them to retire.

"Prior to the market adjustments of summer 1998, the trend for a number of years had been to return capital," says an industry observer. "But, once the hedge fund world digested the losses associated with the market turmoil, people went on a binge to raise capital. Many managers thought that if they did not raise capital, they would run the risk of losing investors."

PATRIARCHS OF THE HEDGE FUND WORLD

Fund managers, including Leon Levy and Jack Nash of Odyssey Partners, Louis Moore Bacon of Moore Capital Management Inc., Paul Tudor Jones of Tudor Management, and George Soros of Soros Fund Management, have all returned capital to investors. The situation always seems to be the same: The managers have decided that they will be unable to continue to post as superior returns with the sums of money they have and therefore do not want to risk their performance record with too much money to manage.

In some cases, like Michael Steinhardt as well as Nash and Levy, the managers decided that there was more to managing money than they were willing to do at this time and that the best thing to do was to close up shop. While others have decided to give back portions of their assets and continue investing as they have for many years to come, these people decided to get out of the business and pass the torch to relatives or friends.

There have also been a number of instances when fund managers have decided that there's so much opportunity out there that they need to get back some of the money they returned, and so reversed course.

One of the most interesting people to have the left the hedge fund community in the past few years is Michael Steinhardt. He got started in the late 1960s with two partners, Howard Berkowitz and Jerold Fine. In the fund's first 14 months of operation it grew 139 percent. By 1970, it had become the nation's largest hedge fund, with over $150 million under management, according to a Securities and Exchange Commission report on the industry. The report was detailed in May 1971 in a story in *Fortune* magazine written by Wyndham Robertson, the sister of Julian Robertson. Titled "Hedge Fund Miseries," the article says "the fund was the only large fund whose assets rose in the period surveyed by the SEC."

At the time, Steinhardt, Fine, and Berkowitz attributed the rise entirely to performance and not to capital infusion. Other funds, according to Wyndham Robertson, saw a decline in assets under management. Some funds lost as much as 95.4 percent of their assets while others lost as little as 1.2 percent.

In 1995, after more than a decade of threatening, Steinhardt finally called it quits. He says that he did not want to be "an armchair philanthropist" and that he wanted to be active in his pursuits apart from money management. Those pursuits range from horticulture and exotic animals to collecting art and providing ways to pass on secular Jewish values to others through organizations.

Until 1994, his fund had never had a down year. Then his wrong bet on European bonds caused his funds to lose close to a billion dollars in assets under management.[12] At the time he announced that he was closing up shop, one industry observer told *The New York Times,* "He recovered beautifully from 1994, so no one can say Michael Steinhardt quit because he could not cut it."[13] A $1,000 investment with Steinhardt from inception to the date it closed its doors in 1995 would have been worth $462,224.

Steinhardt, Soros, Robertson, Tudor Jones, Bacon, and a number of others have built their businesses into so-called super hedge funds. They have proved that no matter how large they get or what type of turmoil rocks the markets, they have the ability to make money.

Still, there has been some question in the past few years whether some of these super hedge funds have become more asset gatherers than traders, simply because the fees (about 1 percent) they earn for dollars under management are so huge.

The Soros organization, which managed $28 billion (prior to the losses in 1998 and 1999), earned approximately $280 million in management fees alone, before it was paid its 20 percent of the profits it earned on its investments.

According to Druckenmiller, the firm's flagship Quantum Fund was up approximately 19 percent for the first eight months of 1998. This being the case, the Soros organization's slice of the pie would have been around a billion dollars.[14]

Obviously, the majority of fund managers earn nowhere near that kind of money. But think of it this way: If a fund has between $50 million and $100 million under management and it charges 1 percent plus 20, the manager stands to gross between $500,000 and $1 million just by showing up for work. If managers show up to work and perform, the revenue they can earn from their funds is nearly endless. It is no wonder Wall Streeters are flocking to the hedge fund world.

When the press and others start to question the fees that funds collect instead of explaining why they should be so high, the fund managers start to perform. As fast as the managers report their numbers to anyone who will take them, the stories switch from complaints about fees to questions about how the managers are able to do so well and regularly beat the market.

Before all the negative stories about Long-Term Capital, one of the most awful pieces of journalism about hedge funds ran in the April 1, 1996, issue of *Business Week*. The article, titled "The Fall of the Wizard of Wall Street—Tiger: The Glory Days Are Over," was about Julian Robertson. In the piece, *Business Week* accused Robertson of not being able to put up good numbers and of viciously attacking his underlings with his hot temper and erratic management style. The article also accused Robertson of not making company visits and not having an active role in the day-to-day management of his funds.[15]

An outraged Robertson responded in two ways. First he posted solid numbers for the year, beating the benchmark S&P substantially; and second he filed a $1 billion libel lawsuit against the magazine and its editors. In a settlement, which was reached in December 1997, *Business Week* was forced to say that its predictions regarding Tiger's investment performance had not been borne out and that it had made a mistake in reporting that Robertson no longer made company visits.[16]

Business Week did not retract its comments about his erratic behavior. Although the altercation proved embarrassing for the magazine in light of the media debacles of 1998, the incident proved to have a relatively minor effect on Robertson's organization.

Most people believe Robertson's vindication came not through the settlement but rather by the performance his funds achieved. His trouncing of the market's benchmarks seemed to prove that the entire thesis of the article was wrong. His returns of over 56 percent for the year showed the world that not only was he still in the game but he was better than ever. And investors took heed; by the end of 1997, Robertson's Ocelot fund had raised over a billion dollars of new money.

Other managers have acted similarly when faced with questions about their ability to manage money and the fees they get for doing it.

Michael Steinhardt told me that one of the things that bothered him the most when he retired was the press's reporting that he did not have a "high-water mark," or a clause in the partnership agreement that says if the fund loses money, the manager will not be paid the incentive fee until it recoups the partners' losses. Steinhardt's fund did not have this clause in the agreement, and the press spent a lot of time writing about that fact when he reported that the fund had lost money for the first time and then announced its subsequent closure.

"While it may now be common industry practice to have a high-water mark, frankly there was no such thing as common industry practices back in 1962," he says. "Hedge funds were not an industry like people talk about them today. It struck me as a bit unfair that the only time the high-water mark issue came up was in 1994, the one year I lost money, 27 years after I started my fund."

Steinhardt says, "There are two sides of a coin. Anybody after a year can leave, and if you stay in when someone is down you are in essence saying that you believe in the manager. You do not make the judgment based on if the fund manager has a high-water mark or not;

you make it based on if you believe in the manager and their investment abilities. My performance record after 27 years in the business stands up as a testament to what I achieved; my business should not have been blackened by some nuance of the partnership agreement."

As many famous hedge fund managers retire and move into more active private lives, a new group of Midas traders is emerging. These men and women are beginning to stake their claim and make their fortune in the industry.

People like Jeffrey Vinik, the dethroned king of the Fidelity Magellan mutual fund, started a hedge fund in 1996 and in his first year made an astounding 100 percent. His fund went from $800 million under management to $1.6 billion. In late 1998, the fund had over $2 billion under management. Many believe his success was made possible because his hands were not tied by regulations that were placed on him when he managed Magellan.

Imagine what would have happened if Vinik had been able to perform as well as the manager of Magellan as he did with his own fund. Not only would there have been a lot more happy investors but most likely Vinik would not have been able to earn as much money. At Fidelity, he did not earn as lucrative an incentive fee nor did he have such a substantial stake in the fund. While on his own, he has both.

Other hedge fund comers who will no doubt reach great heights include Andrew Fisher, formerly of Salomon Brothers, and Cliff Asness, formerly of Goldman Sachs. Even a manager of Harvard University's endowment, Jon Jacobson, has gone out and started his own fund. Unlike some of the younger fund operators, these former "Masters of Their Own Universe" are able to attract large sums of money from the start—making their new business ventures very lucrative right from the get-go.

It was reported that when Jacobson left Harvard, he took with him not only his money but also a check for $500 million of the endowment to manage for the university. Out of the gate he was making $5 million—not including his incentive fee. In Vinik's first year of operation, his firm's total pay package is estimated at over $168 million. Not bad for an operation that has fewer than 50 people working for it.

With all this money at stake, it's no wonder that hedge fund managers catch the blame for the world's financial ills.

HEDGE FUNDS TAKE ALL THE HEAT

Today, both television and print journalists are enamored with hedge funds and with the people who run them. Every time an indicator, be it the Dow Jones Industrial Average or the Thai baht, moves in a direction that is unfavorable to the masses, journalists blame it on hedge funds. In recent years, political leaders have also started to blame hedge fund managers for their countries' market woes.

In 1997 when the Asian currency crisis hit, the first people to be blamed were not the central bankers or the corporate leaders, but the men and women who run private investment partnerships in the United States and abroad.

This was also the case in 1992 when a crisis occurred with the exchange rate mechanism of the European monetary system. It also happened in 1994 when international bond markets went into a tailspin. With each crisis there is blame and in each case the blame was placed on hedge fund operators. Journalists and government leaders alike blamed hedge fund managers for wreaking havoc for the simple benefit of posting higher returns.

It is extremely hard to prove that the hedge funds are a cause of these financial disruptions. A number of studies have been published recently that show that, except in one or two cases, when a hedge fund was blamed for a financial crisis it was not at fault. Most of the time it is the hedge fund that gets caught in the middle—although, in light of the Federal Reserve's action regarding Long-Term Capital, many would find this argument hard to believe.

Case in point: In the summer of 1998, the Russian markets nosedived. Many people believe it was caused by the Asian crisis while others thought the causes were corruption and the inability successfully to move to a capitalist market system. In the early part of the crisis, in the last week of August, the investment manager of the largest hedge fund organization in the world announced that his funds had lost over $2 billion in Russia. Subsequently, many managers came out of the closet and publicly announced that they had lost significant amounts of capital because of the crisis. Although these announcements came as a surprise to many and offered a rare glimpse into the profits and losses of some the world's most successful money managers, for the most part people did not seem to care. Some people were probably happy and believed that these Midas traders got what they deserved.

If these men and women were so powerful that they could control currencies and markets, wouldn't they do so all the time so that they could always make money? No matter how much or how little money one has, no one likes to lose it. If the funds could truly control currencies or manipulate the markets, these massive losses would not have occurred. Instead, these Midas traders were reduced to mere mortal status and joined the ranks of countless other money managers who have made mistakes and proved that they are truly only human.

The *Economist* magazine believes the reason hedge funds catch flak for all of the world's financial crises is ignorance.[17]

The so-called "buccaneers," "gunslingers," and "highwaymen of the global economy" have been blamed for everything from the fracturing of Europe's exchange rate mechanism in 1992 and the crash of the Mexican peso in 1994 to the destabilization of East Asia's currencies in 1997 and the collapse of the Russian ruble in 1998.

Although hedge funds as an industry were attacked for these misfortunes, one person in particular was singled out by a number of finance ministers as being the sole reason for the most recent currency crisis: George Soros.

Headlines around the world cited Soros Fund Management as the reason for the collapse of the Thai baht and other Asian currencies. Malaysian prime minister Mahathir Mohamad blamed Soros and "his Jewish counterparts for getting together and deciding which country's economy to destroy." According to press accounts, the prime minister believes Soros et al. achieve these goals by simply making trades that they know will cause this to happen. The problem with this theory is that hardly anybody besides the prime minister subscribes to it.

Soros and his colleagues were vindicated by a report issued by the International Monetary Fund as well as by statements by then U.S. Secretary of the Treasury Robert Rubin. During a four-nation tour of Asia in the summer of 1998, Rubin said that he did not blame speculators for the Asian financial crisis and that he opposed controls that some countries had urged to restrict their activities. "The role of the speculators will be found to have been relatively small and transient," he says. "I don't think [their trading activity] has been principally or centrally involved in what happened to currencies."[18]

Some believe that Rubin's comments were especially helpful in weakening the growing storm against hedge funds because of his previous role as cochairman and manager of the highly profitable currency trading unit at Goldman Sachs Group LP. "People think he knows about trading and markets because of his former life and they respect what he has to say," says one industry observer. "When someone who used to be in the markets speaks about what is going on in the markets, their voices are heard and their statements for one reason or another always seem to make sense."

The hedge fund world's real vindication came, however, in the form of a study by the International Monetary Fund in the summer of 1998. It made the Malaysian prime minister and those few who subscribed to his beliefs look silly. The report, "Hedge Funds and Financial Market Dynamics," surveyed fund managers over a period of six months, and looked at their trading activities on both a macro and a micro level. Some of its conclusions proved to be the opposite of what was the popular belief regarding the role of hedge funds in currency markets. In most cases, the IMF found that when a hedge fund bet on a currency it brought stabilization to the situation instead of destabilizing it. The study determined that hedge funds were not the only ones to take large positions that bet on the baht's devaluation in 1997. The herd of traders betting on devaluation was led by other commercial and investment banks as well as Thai companies, the report concluded.[19]

The baht situation is not the only currency crisis the IMF reviewed. The study found that many large hedge funds bought substantial positions in the Indonesian rupiah only to lose significant amounts of money when the currency fell from its previous lows.[20] Therefore, the exact opposite of the Malaysian prime minister's remarks seems to be true regarding hedge fund collusion on devaluation of the world currencies.

The IMF study also looked at a number of issues surrounding the most recent financial crises and found that in each episode, the hedge funds seem to have made the situations more stable, not less so. According to the study, because of the "little concrete information" available about the trading patterns of the various hedge funds that were looked at, there is no way to determine what, if any, role they played in these crises. Still, through their efforts to post strong returns they often sell currencies short when a country's macroeconomics look questionable.[21] Although shorting a currency may seem bearish, in reality it is bullish because eventually the position has to be covered by the short seller. If a hedge fund shorts a currency, it is betting on its getting weaker initially. Yet the manager knows that it will have to be bought back, and most likely plans to ride it to new highs on the upside.

The IMF determined that even if the largest hedge funds did all move together or "herd," the scope of their investments would not be anywhere near that of other institutional investors simply because the others have more money.

"The amount of money these macro hedge funds control is relatively small compared to institutional investors," says Barry Eichengreen, one of the authors of the IMF study. "Hedge funds do not stack up against banks, corporations, and pension funds which engage in the exact same kind of speculation. The hedge funds are more vocal and in the spotlight more than multinational corporations or money center banks."

Eichengreen's comments were echoed by former Federal Reserve chairman Paul Volcker. "Hedge funds are a convenient symbol. They move money around fast for quick gains and everybody thinks they are important players in the markets, but in reality they are nothing but a minor factor," he says. "The flows of money come from insurance companies, banks, and other institutions that move from one market to another to cover expenses and make profits. When the markets get upset and become filled with turbulence, it is not the hedge funds' fault; it is the fault of poor economic policy."

No matter how many times Volcker or his peers say it, many still do not believe it, and these nonbelievers continue to blame hedge fund managers for their economic woes.

The carnage of 1998 might have made Volcker's comment clear to many more had the Federal Reserve not been involved with the bailout of Long-Term Capital. The losses that many funds sustained in the wake of the currency and equity crises worldwide were staggering.

GEORGE SOROS—THE WORLD'S GREATEST INVESTOR

To understand how finance ministers around the globe came to the conclusion that hedge funds are to blame, we need to look at where and when the ill will toward hedge funds started. The finger-pointing started in the wake of the devaluation of the British pound in 1992. It was after this incident that George Soros become known as the world's greatest and its most feared investor.

Soros's efforts netted his fund more than $985 million, truly an incredible bet and enough to make him the world's greatest investor. What most people overlook when they discuss this situation, however, is the amount of risk involved in the bet. It is estimated that at the time he put on the trade, he had more than $10 billion at risk. Had he made a mistake, he most likely would have been wiped out. He bet the ranch and he won.

The story begins in 1990 when Great Britain decided to join the new Western European monetary system. At the time, according to Robert Slater's unauthorized biography, *Soros: The Life, Times, and Trading Secrets of the World's Greatest Investor,* Soros did not think it was a good idea for Britain because its economy was not as strong as the new united Germany's and therefore would be at its mercy.

Under the European monetary system agreement, Britain was to maintain its exchange rate of £2.95 to the German mark. As its economy continued to get worse, the pound faced increasing pressure, but because of the agreement, Britain was unable to move. Throughout the summer of 1992, John Major's Tory government assured the world that the pound would recover and that devaluation was not an option.

Soros, according to Slater, thought this to be nonsense and believed that the situation was a lot worse than the Conservatives thought. By mid-September, the Italians, facing mounting economic pressures of their own, devalued the lira, albeit within agreement guidelines. This was the beginning of the end for the system's ability to determine exchange rates. The actions by the Italians set in motion the trade that has made the name George Soros known in all corners of the world.

On September 15, 1992, Major's government announced that Britain was pulling out of the European rate mechanism and in turn devaluing the pound. The news rocked currency markets around the globe. Traders were sent running to cover their positions in a desperate effort to limit losses. One trader, however, was laughing all the way to the bank. Before the announcement, Soros had sold $10 billion in sterling. When the news broke, his hedge fund racked up almost $1 billion in profit. One trade, one man, one hedge fund.

From that point on, the world has never looked at hedge funds or George Soros in the same way again. The world now saw these once-obscure investment vehicles as forces to be reckoned with—traders who had the Midas touch.

Chapter 3

The Managers

I t is now time to meet some hedge fund managers. These are people from all across Wall Street who have decided that they no longer want to work for a brokerage firm or investment bank but would rather pursue an entrepreneurial existence. Ten unique managers are profiled in this chapter—managers who for the most part you will not read about in *The Wall Street Journal* or the popular press. These managers all use a different investment style and I believe are a good representation of the industry. The idea behind choosing these people is to illustrate the depth of talent in the hedge fund world—and to provide examples of how various managers operate their funds and what types of strategies they employ to have solid performance while working to preserve capital.

The following pages tell the stories of 10 fund managers from all aspects of the industry. A few readers may know some of them, because they have been around for a number of years, but the managers all have one thing in common: They fly below the press's radar screen. For the most part, these men and women are not called for comments or interviews when a crisis breaks or a boom hits. In some cases it is the first time the manager has agreed to be interviewed. Although each focuses on a different field of investment and their assets range from $2 million to just under $1 billion, they all have the same goals—to preserve capital and let profits run.

STEVE WATSON

Steve Watson of Watson Investment Partners has everything he possesses tied up in his hedge fund. A native of Arkansas, he has been working on Wall Street since 1987. He started in Texas and after getting an MBA at New York University's Stern School of Business, he worked for Bankers Trust and Friess Associates' Brandywine Mutual Fund before starting his own hedge fund in October 1995.

The fund has a single clear objective: to "beat the Nasdaq composite by investing in small-cap companies." To date things have been working out quite well. After being open for just three years, the fund had a compounded return of 12.5 percent while the Nasdaq was up just 1.45 percent for the same period. The results for 1996 and 1997 were also quite impressive; Watson was up 160 percent and 61.18 percent respectively, while the Nasdaq finished those years up just 22.72 percent and 21.63 percent. By year-end 1997, Watson had an impressive 371.5 percent gross compounded return since inception. At the end of 1998, the fund was up over 37 percent—a quite impressive feat when compared to the Russell 2000, which lost 2.55 percent of its value for the same period. Through the third quarter of 1999, Watson was up 29.26 percent versus 1.3 percent for the Russell 2000 index.

"We have worked and continue to work very hard to put up good numbers," he says from his office on Hedge Fund Row in midtown Manhattan. "In order for us to continue on this trend we are constantly calling companies, meeting with management, and performing research to find the undiscovered companies out there."

The fund invests primarily in companies with a market cap of less than $300 million. It has a turnover rate between 300 percent and 500 percent annually and usually consists of more than 100 stocks. Because of the nature of the stocks Watson buys, he rarely has a position equal to more than 3 percent of assets under management, and for the most part keeps positions to the 1 to 2 percent range. He also carries short positions, which he limits to 2 percent of assets. At the end of 1998, the fund had assets under management of $59 million, which climbed to $102 million in 1999. Watson wants to reach $300 million by the end of the century.

His style is very much like that of legendary mutual fund manager Peter Lynch. In fact, Watson is so enamored with the Fidelity Investments guru that he says he has read Lynch's book *One Up on Wall Street* more than 10 times.

He looks at a universe of over 12,000 small-cap companies that trade on Nasdaq. He believes the key to his success is the ability to find undiscovered companies or out-of-favor companies that have good potential.

"My idea of picking a stock is one that includes understanding the company, understanding the management style and products, and getting a feel for competition," he says. "The only way to truly find a good investment is do work, and by work I mean research and meeting with management."

Watson, who was born in 1964, is from a family that never read *The Wall Street Journal* and hardly knew what a stock was. His father is in the fire and medical alarm business and his mother is a schoolteacher. He got his first taste of Wall Street in an economics course at the University of Arkansas. After graduation, he moved to Dallas, the only big city he had ever been to, and got a job working as a stockbroker at Dean Witter Reynolds in October 1987. On the day the market crashed, Watson picked up his biggest client.

"I found a guy that had not invested in the market and therefore still had all his money," he recalls. "Everyone else had lost their money and had nothing to give to me."

After two years, he decided that he hated selling but loved picking stocks, and moved to New York. He worked at an insurance company as a credit analyst for two more years and completed two-thirds of the chartered financial analyst exam, then decided to go to business school. Initially, New York University's Stern School of Business rejected him, so he started at Fordham University's business school with a plan to transfer to New York University after a semester. Once he entered NYU, he went full time for a year and a half and then took a job at *Individual Investor* magazine, where he wrote about small-cap stocks.

When he finished graduate school, he got a job with Bankers Trust as an analyst for aggressive growth portfolios specializing in small-cap and mid-cap growth companies. After two years, he went to Friess Associates as an analyst for the Brandywine funds.

"I worked at Friess for about a year and a half and I realized that I could pick stock as well as anybody in the country and decided to start my own fund," he says. "I started the fund with about $700,000 from friends, family, and a number of CEOs and CFOs and I had no fear."

The rest, as they say, is history. The fund has been doing very well, both in performance and in its ability to attract new investment dollars.

"I believe that I have as good numbers as anybody in the country that is doing what we are doing, and I know we have one of the best research teams around," he says. "We focus on companies with $300-million-and-under markets and we basically do all of our own research. Our policy is to talk to 20 companies a day, and I know for a fact that not many other funds come anywhere near that number. We have a very good system. We learn about the company, call them, and then load up the calendar and meet them face-to-face."

Watson believes the key to the fund's success is its research. When they talk to a company they try to find out as much as possible in order to make what they believe is a good investment decision. They ask questions that include:

Who is doing well?

Who is getting orders?

Who is losing business?

What new products does a company have?

What new products do its competitors have?

"We are constantly and continuously doing our own research and very rarely use any sell-side research at all," he says. "We are trying to get out in front of the crowd and find undiscovered stocks that people don't know anything about or that have fallen out of favor with the Street."

There are approximately 12,000 public companies with under $300 million market capitalization, and all Watson wants to do is find 1 percent of them that are worthy of his investment dollars.

"If 99 percent of the companies are dogs and we can find 1 percent that we like, then we can make some money," he says. "In a lot of cases there is not research coverage or there is very little and we are competing against retail brokers who don't really know what they are doing. We are trying to buy companies before people know about them and sell them to people once the companies are discovered." One of Watson's first signals to get out of a company is when an analyst starts to cover it.

Watson turns his portfolio quite often based on the risk-reward ratio of the names he is carrying at any given time. His theory is that if he buys a stock that he thinks has an 80 percent upside, and then it moves and has only 20 percent upside, he will sell it and replace it with another stock that has an 80 percent upside. He is constantly trying to keep the risk-reward ratio in check.

Another reason he turns the portfolio so often is because of the nature of the investments. He believes all small-cap stocks will, without a doubt, have some sort of hiccup in an 18-month period. So once a month he reevaluates the stocks in the portfolio and decides how large or small a position he wants to hold in any particular name.

"If a company misses one order, they will miss a number and the stock will get hammered and they can have one bad month, which can really affect their business a lot," he says. "I don't like dead money. I want to be in companies that are doing well right now."

Because Watson rarely puts more than 2 percent of the fund's assets into a single name, he needs to have a lot of them do well. Even if one or two of the stocks become three- or four-baggers (tripling or quadrupling in price) he still is only going to be able to add 4 percent to his bottom line.

"I need to have a lot of winners for the fund to continue to be up as significantly as we have been over the past three years," he says. "It is our only risk, because if a stock really tanks it will only put a dent in our performance. It is a numbers game for us; risk-reward—it is a great system for us and as long as we implement it, we will continue to do well."

Since inception the fund has hit a lot of singles, doubles, and triples (stocks that increased 100 percent, 200 percent, and 300 percent) and has sold a lot of stocks that have gone up tenfold.

"If you look at our philosophy, a lot of times we will buy a stock at $10 that has 10 times earnings and then it hits $20 and the earnings have not changed; we need to sell that stock and buy something else that fits our criteria," he says. "To have a stock that goes up five or six times, we need to continuously upgrade what our earnings estimates are and in a small-cap field it's awfully hard to find a company that does not have a lot of glitches. Plus by the time the stock has gone up 10 times, the company most likely is a billion-dollar company and everyone else knows about it and it is time for us to move on and buy something else."

Before he decides to buy a stock Watson looks at a number of factors like insider buying, new highs, and earnings. Sometimes, he will go through the letters of the alphabet and look up all the companies on the Nasdaq that start with a specific letter.

"With over 12,000 companies out there to choose from it is impossible to hit them all, but we are trying," he says.

One piece of research that Watson finds indispensable is talking to management of the companies. In most cases, Watson and his staff have no problem getting the chief executive officer (CEO) or the chief financial officer (CFO) of a company on the phone.

"I cannot call the chief financial officer of IBM and get him on the phone, and if I did get him on the phone he would not tell me anything of value anyway; but when I call these small companies, not only can I get the CFO, but he is willing to spend time with me on the phone and tell me what is going on," he says. "If they don't get their story out, nobody is going to find them and when they own a good piece of the company, they want their stock to go up. We have very little trouble talking to management."

Watson treasures his ability to communicate with the companies in which he is investing. He knows that if the stock is down 10 percent on a given day, he can call up management and find out what is going on.

"A lot of these guys love to talk because no one else is calling them. In most cases we are all in the same boat: They are trying to build a business and I am trying to build a business," he says.

Besides looking at companies that are new to the marketplace, Watson also looks at turnaround opportunities. In 1997 and 1998 two turnaround stocks that worked well for the fund were Jonestown America and Shoney's Restaurants.

"Both of these stocks got hammered by the Street but we saw some real value in them," he says. "Shoney's in particular—everyone has heard of Shoney's but nobody wanted to eat there. It was not known for its food but rather for being open late. Management decided to upgrade the food and things started to turn around. For us it was the perfect turnaround opportunity—all the bad news was out there and you could buy the stock at three times cash flow."

Watson initially bought Shoney's at $3.25 a share, rode it up to $5 a share, and bought some more. The stock had previously hit a high of $25 before the bad news broke and Watson believed it could go to $10. At $10 it would be a double and that would be all right with him.

The fund also uses short positions to add points to the bottom line. Watson looks to short companies that have become Wall Street's darlings overnight but have no numbers or products to back up the story.

"A stock that has gone from $2 to $20 and is worth a dollar based on our research is a stock we would short," he says. "[We would short] companies that may have good earnings but, if you look behind the earnings, may have a negative cash flow. We don't short stocks based purely on valuation, because expensive stocks tend to get more expensive and I don't want any shorts to hurt us in a big way."

The fund usually closes out its short positions once it makes 50 percent, and moves on to the next company. One stock it did not do that with is International Precious Metals. Watson shorted the stock in 1997 at $8 and at the time we first met for this piece of the book in April 1998 still owned it at 50 cents.

The story behind the stock is that the company told the world that it had a huge gold deposit in Nevada and had a study that proved it. The problem with the stock was that the state of Nevada had done its own study and found no gold. The company rebutted the state's finding, saying its study proved that the gold was there, and the stock went up. The bubble burst when someone discovered that the study the company was using was done in a high school geology class.

"The whole thing turned out to be a fraud," says Watson. "We just shorted it and knew it was going to go down. The tough thing with shorts is making sure you don't get bought in." When a fund is bought in, it means that the broker forces the buyer to cover his position.

In January 1997, Watson wrote in his monthly newsletter about a stock that he thought would be a great short. The problem was he could not get any. None of his brokers could borrow the stock and so he was not able to make any money when the stock nose-dived.

His research was simple. He called the company, asked for samples of its products, and gave the products to some friends to test. None of them would recommend it.

"It was the perfect situation. Not one of the people I asked to try out the product said that they would ever buy it, let alone use it," he says. "What a great short. The company was burning cash left and right and talking a great story on Wall Street, but when it comes down to it, if nobody is going to buy the product, then it is going to get killed."

The stock went from $20 to 50 cents in 12 months.

"It is all a relationship game because you need to be able to borrow the shares and keep them," he says. "You need to be able to stay with the position once you identify it and not worry about being bought in."

Watson does most of the fund's trading through two firms where he believes the strength of his relationship allows him to get the best execution.

"Because we don't have an in-house trader, we use two traders that are good friends that know how we like to get filled and work the orders like it was their own money," he says. "When you have 100 stocks in the portfolio, you are always buying this, selling that, rotating money around—very much like what Peter Lynch did with Magellan. We are not interested in buying 10 stocks and seeing what happens; we are constantly trying to maximize returns."

Watson believes his success rests in the amount of work he and his colleagues do to find solid investment ideas. They do all of their own research.

"Most small-cap managers don't do as much work as we do," he says. "I don't think that they call on nearly as many companies as we do. There are at least 12,000 companies out there and most managers probably don't call on more than three companies a day and we are talking to 20. We have to have seven times as many good ideas as they have simply because we are talking to more people."

Watson would like to build his business to include other funds. He believes that once he gets $200 million to $300 million under management, he will need to launch new products to maximize returns. He would like to start a fund that invests in mainstream stocks and possibly one that invests in private placements.

"There is really a need in the marketplace for funds that can take advantage of the type of investments that we are looking for, and the reality of the situation is that there is a lot of room for us to grow, both in and out of the small-cap market," he says.

HANYA KIM

Hanya Kim is relatively new to the hedge fund business. The 33-year-old started her fund, Intrepid International Group LLC, in late 1997. It focuses on emerging markets and looks for investments in the undiscovered areas of the world that are off Wall Street's radar screen. For most of 1998, Kim was focused on investing in Bulgaria. Of all the former Eastern bloc countries, Kim found Bulgaria to offer the most unusual investment opportunities. She has invested in everything from chemical plants to cigarette manufacturers. Most of her ideas come from being on the ground and as such she spends a lot of time flying to and from New York in order to stay on top of her investments and to find new opportunities.

Kim got started on Wall Street after graduating in just two years from Maryland's Towson State University in 1986. She completed her undergraduate work quickly by taking "a lot of classes and attending summer school."

"I did not particularly like undergraduate work," she says. "It was sort of tedious; they don't let you study what you want to study. Instead, you have to take a number of requirements. I had two options, either to drop out or to graduate early, and I chose to graduate early."

After talking to a number of graduate schools, she decided to travel and see the world. She ended up moving to Korea after graduation to enroll in a language course. Although her father is Korean, she had never learned the language and decided while in school to do so. While in Korea, she landed a job as an equity analyst for Sanmil Accounting.

"It was a really great time to be there," she recalls. "It was right at the time when they were making the change from dictatorship to democracy."

At Sanmil, she learned how to analyze markets and look at companies. She spent three years in Korea and then came back home to Johns Hopkins University's Nitze School of Advanced International Studies.

At Johns Hopkins she did a double major in international economics and military strategy. "I had always found military strategy interesting and while I was in Korea, I spent a lot of time talking about U.S. security policy," she says. "I always liked Russia and Eastern Europe and I realized while I was in Korea that I wanted to either start a fund or continue being an analyst; and although I knew that it would not necessarily lead to it, I had spoken to some alumni who had studied sort of what they wanted and were still able to get a job on Wall Street."

Kim was hired at insurer American International Group Inc. (AIG) as a management trainee. Although she wanted to go to the investment side, the theory at the company was that in order to invest money, one first had to know where the money came from. After spending a few months in Delaware in the insurance accounting department, Kim moved to New York as an assistant portfolio manager.

"I worked with two people who really did not like me very much," she says. "One in particular—we were always fighting; it was really horrible."

It turned out that Kim had been set up. She had been sent to New York to train under and eventually replace one of the people she was working with. At first, Kim thought she was going to lose her job because of all the fighting but quickly realized that was not the case.

"We basically worked like dogs; we did everything from investing in Trinidad and Tobago to buying U.S. mortgage securities," she recalls.

In most cases when a company has a local insurance operation, it is required to invest some of the money locally, so Kim and her colleagues were constantly trying to find investments throughout the four corners of the earth.

"We would often buy some government bonds and then in order to pick up some yield take some money and invest in direct equity," she says. "In the Caribbean, what you do is invest in the country's only CAT scan machine or something like that in order to meet our investment requirements."

Kim relied on local investment personnel and a lot of grunt work to come up with ideas as well as perform due diligence and research.

"I spent a lot of time on the ground, meeting with people. Everyone has a deal; the skill is to weed out the good from the bad and make the determination without putting too much capital at risk," she says. "We always looked for investment with hard-currency revenue streams."

Kim left AIG in 1994 to work at Global Advanced Technology Corp. as a consultant focusing on the mortgage derivative market. She specialized in providing risk analysis on emerging market debt and equity strategies.

"After working there for about three years or so, I realized that I was at the point both in the market and in my career for me to leave and start my own fund," she says. "The market was doing really well, which meant it was a good time to raise money."

Kim's initial investments came from former colleagues and business associates. She started the fund with well under $1 million. At first she had a hard time putting the money to work; she could not find solid investments because of the market levels.

"When I first got started, I had sort of hoped the bubble would burst, because although it was easy to raise money it was hard to find good places for it," she says. "The climate has cooled down; now it is easy to find investments and not as easy to raise money."

Kim employs a tandem macro/micro strategy to find investment opportunities. Her macro strategy includes picking a country, studying its government and its economic policies, looking at its relationship to the European Union, and observing what, if any, civil wars happen to be taking place. Once she finds a country, she employs a micro strategy, which includes looking at and analyzing debt and equity investment opportunities.

At the time of our meeting in 1998, Kim's investment focus was on Bulgaria's chemical plants and tobacco companies.

"The key to this region of the world is that privatization tends to bring in a lot of foreign investment, creating a boom-bust cycle. People go crazy throwing money in and the first people in do really well," she says. "For example, in Poland before the institutional money went in, the individual investors that went in made a killing. Now there are too many people there and the edge has been taken off the market."

Kim believes that Bulgaria has a lot to offer. Not only is the government very stable but also its currency had not moved throughout the whole Asian crisis of late 1997 and 1998. Other countries in the region took it on the chin while things in Bulgaria kept the status quo.

She decided to invest in Bulgaria after her macro research determined that it met her guidelines.

"There is a strong political environment with a government that is committed to reform, and it is one of the few countries in the region committed to the European Union and controlling fiscal and monetary sides," she says. "It was one of the few that I found fit my investing criteria really well."

The key to investing in these type of countries is access. Kim equates this region of the world to the Wild West.

"There is no clear structure in place for investment in most cases and in order to be successful you need to be able to have access to high-ranking officials and businesspeople," she says.

Kim has been able to establish these types of ties because of her work at AIG as well as through a number of people she has worked with who are consultants to foreign governments.

"Once you are able to get to talk to people on a certain level, like the deputy minister of finance and the head of the privatization agency, you are able to get some idea of what is going on and can go back and talk to the people in the various industries looking for investments and compare the information," she says. "There is a lot of going back and forth in order to find out who is bullshitting who and what makes sense to look at in terms of investing."

After buying some positions with her initial capital, Kim focused on raising more. In the first quarter of 1998 she was able to increase her fund fourfold to $4 million. She expects to be up to $25 million by the middle of the year 2000.

"I am targeting $25 million for two reasons: one, because it is a raiseable amount, and two, because it will allow me to be quite nimble," she says. "If a big fund looks at a market like Bulgaria, they will have a hard time finding profitable investments, but with $25 million, I can essentially act as an individual investor would, not like a big institution."

She has delegated most of the marketing effort to members of her board of directors. They are concentrating on finding investors on both coasts and in Asia. One of the strengths of her marketing plan, she believes, is her lack of sales skills; it is the first time in her career that she has had to be on the pitch side of the equation. "Marketing is not one of my fortes," she says. "However, without it I will not be able to grow my business to where I want, and therefore I am trying to spend a fair amount of time with it—because as the money comes in, I need to be concentrating on investing the dollars and continuing on posting solid returns."

The returns for the fund have been pretty good. In the first three months of business, Kim posted returns of just over 18 percent. Although it doesn't seem so good when weighted for risk next to, say, the Standard & Poor's 500 stock index, it actually is very strong considering the beating most Eastern European and Asian economies took during the same period and especially in light of the Asian and Russian turmoil.

Because of the nature of her investments, Kim believes the best way to stay on top of them is to be where they are, so she spends about 20 percent of her time in Bulgaria and other countries checking up on investments and looking for new ones.

"I work really closely with a number of people on the ground who really make it fun to go over there," she affirms. "It is quite interesting to watch countries and industries develop literally before your eyes."

The key, however, as at AIG, is weeding out the good from the bad. This process can be difficult, but she believes her background has provided her with the right tools to ask the right questions. She looks at what industries are being privatized, where she sees stumbling blocks, where there are entrenched local interests that will slow the privatization of local industries, and where multilateral institutions are investing money. Of course, she is also then looking for companies that are well run and have some semblance of good management in place:

"Some of the companies have managements that are holdovers from the Communist era who are skimming off the top and don't have an idea of what is going on, while others, including a number of the ones I have invested in, have management that is really good. These firms have been keeping things going on a shoestring and in most cases when they do get a small investment, the management uses the money well. They literally take a small bit of money and run with it, increasing production and efficiency."

At the time of our meeting, Kim was investing as little as $10,000 and as much as $45,000 in various equity, debt, and private placements. If something looked particularly interesting, like tobacco in late

1997, she would split the investment with a number of companies in the industry. Eventually her investment in the Bulgarian tobacco industry was over $150,000.

Kim believes that she will continue to focus on the undiscovered areas of the world, as she believes these provide the best opportunities for success.

"Unless you are completely wired into places like the Hong Kong Jockey Club or have other connections that allow you to find out what is truly going on, Asia is a very tough place to make money," she says. "I prefer to be in an area where there is a level playing field and the institutional money is not."

PETER FAULKNER

Peter Faulkner makes money when other people decide not to do the work or are just plain lazy. As the manager of Rumpere Capital, Faulkner invests in special situations. He is a value investor: He looks for opportunities that are not of the norm. For example, he may buy debt or equity positions in a company on the verge of or in bankruptcy. Simply put, he does his homework, finds the opportunity, and tries to exploit it for a gain.

Faulkner was raised in Italy by an American father and an Italian mother. He went to the Georgetown University School of Foreign Service. In 1983, he took a job as an assistant to Hans Jacobson, who was working with Max Heine at Herzog, Heine, Geduld. He worked with Heine and Jacobson as well as with Michael Price for a number of years, where he learned the art of distressed investing, Faulkner then went to Alex. Brown & Sons, where he developed its distressed investment division, and then in 1992 he decided to work with Martin Whitman of M. J. Whitman Inc. and the Third Avenue funds. The deal he made with Whitman was that he would develop the firm's trading desk but, once the operation was up and running, he would be able to go out on his own. In October 1992, he launched Rumpere. While Faulkner continues to run Rumpere, he also decided to join forces with Whitman to launch another fund that will take advantage of the distressed market. The idea is to be able to make use of both men's operations to draw on their research and investment capabilities.

Pronounced "roomperay," Rumpere is Latin for "broken." The name stems from the phrase "broken beach," which is the predecessor to the word "bankruptcy."

"I launched the vehicle with some of my own money and some high-net-worth individuals' money and sort of piddled around with it for a while because what people referred to as 'hedge funds' had become a much more organized industry," he says. "There were real competitors with real money who had established large organizations with strong track records and I felt I could not compete with those people."

Faulkner felt that with only $7 million under management he would have to establish himself before anyone would take his fund seriously. When pitching to possible investors, he would face established funds that had staff and research abilities.

Meanwhile, it was just him. "I realized that I could not compete as long as I did not have a track record, so I decided to go after a track record," he says. "The key to the whole industry is having a track record and longevity."

Things seem to have gone well in that regard. From his fund's start in 1992 through year-end 1996, Faulkner had in annual return of 23.07 percent. That beat both the S&P 500 and the Merrill Lynch High Yield Index, which came in at 15.22 percent and 12.75 percent respectively. He had strong year in 1997, finishing up 26.2 percent, and things were on track for 1998 going into the summer. However, 1998 did not turn out so well and the fund finished down for the year. Through September, 1999 the fund recovered up 13.6 percent.

In early 1998, Faulkner decided to go on the road and market the fund heavily. He expects to have $40 million to $50 million by year-end 2000 and hopes to build the fund to more than $200 million by year-end 2001.

"This industry has developed like most industries to the point that you can outsource just about anything, except for my brain," he says. "I essentially can operate a fund that large from a small office with a computer because I can outsource all of the back-office functions, transaction processing, and marketing for an infinitely small amount of what it would cost to do it in-house. Now by working with the Whitman shop, I will be able also to take advantage of their research and technology and bring the costs down even lower."

One of the ways Faulkner is raising money is by striking an exclusive deal with a third-party marketing firm. The marketer will not work with another fund focused on distressed investing and Faulkner will not work with any other third-party marketing firm. Faulkner pays the marketer a percentage of the fees he makes from the dollars the firm generates.

"This is a fabulous arrangement for both of us," he says. "It allows me to concentrate on research and investing while they can concentrate on raising money and working the customer relations aspect of the business."

Faulkner considers himself a value investor but with a quirk: He looks for companies in trouble.

"We look for companies where we can identify four key attributes," he says. "The attributes are tangible asset values, good market niche, viable products, and competent management. Once we find these four things, we keep it simple, safe, and cheap."

Faulkner's particular strategy, which causes some people to complain that there is not a lot left to do in distressed investing today, is to find a viable company that is going through temporary problems. He looks for companies that are in the middle of restructuring where research provides quantitative evidence that the bottom has been hit. In some cases, earnings are beginning to improve, and the company has written down excess inventory and the like.

"I prefer to buy a bond at 40 or 50 cents on the dollar and ride it to 80, as opposed to buying it at 10 cents on the dollar where there is a chance that it can go to zero," he says.

Faulkner explains his simple, safe, and cheap methodology as follows:

Simple is defined by what he buys. He likes companies with tangible assets and solid distribution networks as well as situations that do not offer capital structure arbitrage, a technical term for buying the senior bonds and shorting the junior bonds.

Safe is defined by when and where he buys into the company. In most cases, he likes to go in when there is very little uncertainty and when he does buy he gets in at the top of the capital structure.

"If a company has a small tranche of senior notes, meaning it does not have a terribly leveraged balanced sheet, and it is experiencing problems with its business and the stock is down 50 percent, I believe that at that point it is time to buy the common stock," he says. "This is as safe as buying a senior note of a company in bankruptcy, because a senior note of a company in bankruptcy is your future equity; while when you buy the stock you are already there."

Faulkner agrees with those who say there is nothing left to do in distressed stock business because there are not a lot of good companies not yet in bankruptcy that have defaulted on bonds now trading significantly below par. Still, he believes there is a lot to do in niche brand-name companies that have a good market share and good products that have screwed up somewhere. Faulkner believes these companies have made a mistake, the stock is way down, and the company, because it was always a leader in its field, never really leveraged itself. Therefore he can get in and make a killing once things turn around.

Companies that illustrate these kinds of opportunities include Sunbeam, Samsonite, Corporate Express, and PetSmart. All were leaders in their respective industries, but management made mistakes and the companies fell on hard times. Yet once management gets a handle on the situation and starts to turn things around, they each offer extraordinary opportunities.

"There are a lot of those things that once you speak to management, you can see that things have bottomed out and there are some problems left to fix but the company is essentially on its way to getting better," he asserts. "A lot of distressed guys don't buy this kind of stuff because they say it is not what they do. And that is wrong. Just because the company is not in bankruptcy does not mean that there are not good opportunities."

Faulkner defines the cheap portion of his strategy as the intrinsic value. He always tries to buy a business at below the private market valuation of the company and below what he believes to be the liquidation value of the company.

"The best hedge at the end of the day is buying cheap," he says.

One of the most important pieces of the puzzle that Faulkner looks for before buying into something is some sort of major event about to happen. For example, he bought into Corporate Express, an office supply company whose stock had been down over 50 percent, knowing that although the company had planned to increase earnings slowly, the real catalyst for the turnaround was going to be its shedding of noncore assets. Once this took place, the company and its stock would rebound.

Faulkner uses a number of parameters to define cheap. In some cases, he looks at a cash-flow earnings model, which includes looking for a normalization of cash flow. He also looks for the possibility of noncore sales and liquidation values as well as coming up with a value for the company as a private concern. Once he answers these questions, he figures out an inherent value, which is the key to how much the company is worth under a number of scenarios.

"What we basically do is look at a business and decide that it is worth 'x,' and if we can buy the bonds for 50, 60, or 70 percent of 'x' it makes sense to get in because in the long run it will work out," he explains.

In 1998, Faulkner was investing in Alliance Entertainment, Harrahs Jazz Casino in New Orleans, Trans World Entertainment, and a number of European companies. In each case, his research told him that the companies were niche players and that once things turned around each would be strong in its respective field.

"The key to my investment philosophy is that on first look most people don't see the opportunity and are too lazy to do the work to make the determination that it is worth it," he says. "Most of the world does not want to do anything more than look on Bloomberg or Dow

Jones Investor News for information. I don't believe you can find anything of value from these sources. In order to really understand what is going on, you have to call the company, you have to dig; and basically what we do is we make money when other people are too lazy to make the phone calls."

By doing primary research, speaking to management, and reading balance sheets, Faulkner believes he is able to make an informed decision on the strength and weakness of a company.

"I love my job. I equate it to being in college. In college, I took a whole lot of courses and then I took a test and I got an A, a C, or whatever," he says. "This is the same thing. I am a generalist. The industries find us when they are in trouble. We don't go out and say, 'We think the road paving business is overvalued right now.' We don't do that. When the road paving business takes a hit, we look at it. I look at all different types and sizes of companies a day and then I make a decision."

Faulkner finds his opportunities through many information channels, including reading the newspaper and talking to people he knows in and around Wall Street.

"You look at things, you find companies that look interesting, and then you do the work. Your grade is whether you make money or not," he says. "The only difference is that you have other people's money and it is a little more stressful."

Faulkner believes that the reason hedge funds are successful is because of the structure of the payout to management.

"It is very simple. Who would not want to be invested in a company where management owns over 10 percent? They know that management only gets compensated when the stock goes up and then only if they make money—if the stock goes down and if management loses money, it does not get paid until it earns everything back," he says. "What more could a person want from an investment vehicle?

"People who question why management should get 20 percent of profits are better off investing in a mutual fund, which has over a hundred names and the manager most likely does not know everything he owns, and he only makes money based how big his assets are," he continues. "I only make money based on how profitable my assets are."

Faulkner believes everything is driven by human nature and that one reason most people on Wall Street are not successful with distressed investing is that there are very few incentives for the analyst to do the work needed to figure out the situation.

"It is easy to whip out a quick report on a publicly traded company that everyone follows; the company sends out big investor kits and all that kind of stuff that can be done in an afternoon," he says. "This kind of thing is a lot easier than doing what I do; the time of analysis to creating commissions is much less for a big publicly traded company than an illiquid, hard-to-research company."

Faulkner continues, "This is not easy. It takes a certain level of perseverance and diplomacy to do this type of work. It is hard to call up a company that is in trouble and get them to talk to you and do the research. For the most part, companies and their advisers don't want to talk, but, if you have a relationship with the people, you are able to get a feel for what is going on and make a decision accordingly."

The first thing Faulkner looks for when he decides to make an investment is to determine how much he can lose. He is the first to admit that sometimes he makes a mistake, so in case something happens, he wants to know what is truly at stake. For example, he buys a bond at 30 cents on the dollar that he thinks could go to 50 but instead of being worth $200 million, it is now worth $100 million. Many times, he will go in at 30, watch it go to 10, buy more at 10, watch it go to 20, and then sell it all.

"I always look at a company and say, 'It is a leader in its field and it is going to fix its problems,'" he says, "When things get normal again, it should do this and I can buy it at this and therefore it is cheap and something I want to get involved with."

Faulkner believes that once he has assets under management of $200 million to $250 million he will close Rumpere to new investors. He believes those levels are ideal because he will be able to remain flexible—meaning he can put a decent amount of capital (10 percent of the portfolio) to work without raising his level of risk.

RICHARD VAN HORNE AND GUY ELLIOT

Richard Van Horne and Guy Elliot are modern-day explorers. They're like Vasco da Gama and Hernando de Soto, constantly venturing to the far ends of the earth for adventure and treasure. Unlike the Iberians, who sought new routes and new worlds, Van Horne and Elliot are looking for investment opportunities.

The two manage Croesus Capital Management, a $250 million group of hedge funds that invest in everything from oil wells in the former Soviet Union to farm equipment in North Africa. Started in 1993, the funds have posted significant returns by finding unique investment opportunities in the world's emerging markets. As of the spring of 1998, the main fund had posted annual compounded return of approximately 39 percent since inception. However, in light of the collapse of many of the emerging markets as well as the volatility in the Russian debt market, the fund ended 1998 down approximately 40 percent.

"This is the first calendar year we have had terrible results and it really tests people's faith," admits Van Horne. "It has been a troubled year for all kinds of strategies in the emerging markets, whether they are regional or industry specific. It is going to be hard sailing for a few years.

"We are not thriving but we are doing more than surviving," he continues. "A lot of our investors who have been with us for a lot of years expect us to make them back a lot of money, and we expect to make it back for them."

As a result of the losses, the fund family has seen some investors redeem their capital and expects redemptions to continue until the emerging markets stabilize.

"A lot of our clients are in a fund of funds, and if the investor takes his or her money out of the fund of funds, it has to redeem its position with us," says Van Horne. "Some of our investors have entire portfolios in hedge funds and have seen the value of their entire portfolios drop. In some cases people are selling everything in order to determine how much cash they can raise."

The Croesus organization consists of four funds, all designed to invest in distinct emerging opportunities. One fund operates in a merchant banking capacity in Central Europe, another focuses on low-volatility debt in local currencies, a third invests solely in Russia's public and private equity markets, and the fourth specializes in emerging market stock of natural resource companies.

The firm's philosophy is that the market as a whole does not understand the risk of investing in economies in transition. If you can get a handle on the risk, which includes understanding political as well economic situations, these environments often present very profitable investment opportunities.

"Economies that are in transition represent major opportunities," says Elliot. "Capital-deprived markets offer excess returns in order to attract investors. In most cases, markets with favorable policy environments will attract capital, and fundamentals will win out."

In light of the turmoil that rocked the Russian debt and equity markets, the fund had significant losses in its Russia-only fund. The fund lost over 90 percent of its assets under management due to performance and redemptions. However, after the dust settled, Croesus reevaluated its positions and has decided to continue its investments in the area.

"Russia is still on the outs and it seems like only the brave are still there," says Van Horne. "We believe in the region and will continue to build up positions in the country while taking advantage of pricing discrepancies to allow us to make favorable returns from the investments. In a sense Russia is on the verge of being uninvestable as it was in 1994 when we started investing over there, making it exactly the kind of market we like."

Given what has happened, Croesus has realized that it no longer needs to own 20 stocks in the portfolio. Instead it has chosen five or six names, stocks that are first-tier stocks that over time Croesus believes will provide significant returns.

"The investors were not overjoyed by what happened, but I think the view was, 'The fund was worth this much at one time, way up here'—and not that it is worth this much, down here—'so why should I sell it?' " says Van Horne. "Many investors felt that the money is already there and it is not that easy; the managers are below the high-water mark, so if it is going to go back up all of the capital gains would go to the investor."

Van Horne and Elliot work with a team of eight investment professionals who scour the globe. In most cases, the firm works with people on the ground in the various places where they are or are considering investing. By having people in place, they are able to ensure that they get the best possible access to information and are able to find new opportunities as they arise.

"Our partners enable us to have access to streams of information in order to find opportunities and perform research to make investment decisions," says Elliot. "Without our network of partners and contacts in the various areas of the world we are looking at to invest in, our job would be much harder and we would not be able to perform as well."

The firm's strategy is to determine where the best risk-adjusted returns are while finding major themes, such as regions of the world, industries, or specific companies to invest in. Once they make these decisions, they evaluate market fundamentals. This step includes looking at macroeconomic and political trends as well as microtechnical analysis. Once all of these steps are taken and the investment criteria are met, they construct a portfolio. The managers evaluate market segments and time horizons as well as the allocation of capital based on the ability to earn high risk-adjusted total returns. The portfolio is constructed to capitalize on political, economic, and social changes while being aware of the need to protect the capital base.

When Elliot and Van Horne launched Croesus, they operated out of a small room in an office suite across from Grand Central terminal in New York. Now the firm occupies an entire floor in the old CS First Boston building in midtown Manhattan. Although things have changed in terms of money under management and the office space and staffing requirements, the funds' investment style has pretty much stayed the same. The only difference is that now they are investing much greater sums in many more places.

Van Horne met Elliot in 1992 when he was working with a specialized investment management company fund called FondElec

Group Inc., based in Connecticut, that was started to invest in electricity privatization in Latin America. At the time he was also operating a small fund, the Emerging Markets Total Return Fund LP, with just under $500,000, in which Elliot had invested. In the first quarter of 1993, Van Horne got a call from Elliot asking him to invest in a fund he was starting. When the paperwork arrived, he realized they should be in business together.

"When I looked at the private placement memo and his investment rationale outline, I thought it was very similar to what I was planning to do in order to grow my fund," he says. "I called him back and said that we should do something together because there was really no point to invest in each other's funds if we were going after the same opportunities."

Elliot, who is English, got involved with investing in emerging markets while working at Cargill, Inc. He spent 12 years there, worked at Merrill Lynch, and started a hedge fund with some ex-Cargill colleagues before he decided to go out on his own.

Van Horne learned about the emerging markets while working for J. P. Morgan in Tokyo and New York. He realized after a stint as an institutional salesman at Merrill Lynch that he wanted to be on the other side of the phone and that selling was not a way to build a future.

At the time they joined forces on June 4, 1993, they had $1.4 million under management. A mutual friend offered them a room in his suite of offices as long as they paid for the Reuters machine and the phone lines.

"We were very fortunate that at the time we started, the emerging markets really began to take off," Van Horne says. "We made some good calls in both the debt and equity markets so that by the time investors started to make allocations, we had seven months of solid performance."

Also helping was the fact that then there were very few small emerging market funds, so they didn't face the crowding-out effect that many funds face today.

By January 1994, funds under management had risen to $70 million. At that point, the two decided to stop taking new investment dollars because they wanted to be sure that they had an organization that would allow them to manage the money successfully and to operate efficiently.

"We were lucky to be in the right place at the right time," says Van Horne.

Since 1994, Croesus has grown from two people to 25, eight of whom are on the investment team and the rest working on client services and management.

As the firm has evolved and the principals have thought about the markets, they have developed certain themes that they like to follow. The idea is to build on accumulated knowledge and experience.

At the time we met to discuss Croesus, half of the firm's money was in the main Emerging Markets Total Return Fund and the rest was in the smaller funds.

"This business model has allowed us to increase our investment team, because as we add these separate pools of money we are able to collect fees, and the base management fees are able to fund our day-to-day operation while the incentive fee at the end of the year pays us and our people."

Van Horne believes that Croesus has "quite a lot of firepower" when it comes to its investment professionals.

One of the smaller pools Croesus operates is its Russia fund, started when it was just a two-man shop.

"At the time, we saw Russia as a very unique investment opportunity," Van Horne says. "Now four years later, things have completely changed and as such we have adjusted the style of our investing. Instead of managing the pool of money from New York, we now have an office in Moscow with six investment professionals as part of a joint venture with United Financial Group, which is the leading independent investment banking firm there."

United Financial was started by Boris Fyodorov, who was twice minister of finance and once deputy prime minister of Russia. The partnership with United Financial allows Croesus to have people on the ground constantly looking for and managing investments. Elliot equates the climate of investing in Russia to an onion.

"There are many layers to the financial community currently in Russia. There are some who are very close to the center while there are others on the fringe, and the key to success is to be able to peel away as many layers as possible in order to get a clear picture of what is going on and invest accordingly," says Elliot. "Our relationship with United Financial Group evolved similarly to that of mine and Richard's. I was standing on the balcony with them in Moscow discussing our direction and it became clear that it was very much like theirs, and we decided that we could do it better together than on our own."

After months of determining a structure for the operation, the two firms joined forces. Elliot and Van Horne's approach to emerging markets is to try to get inside the market, anywhere that they are really interested in being involved.

"You have to be true to yourself when you are investing, and if you are not, the market will reveal that you wear no clothes. For us being true to ourselves means getting under the surface and a depth of involvement that gives us a comfort level with what we are investing in," says Elliot. "We can't just sit back and read the broker reports and say that makes and this doesn't make sense—that is superficial. We have always been sort of early-stage emerging market investors, and that means that you have to do your own legwork."

What drives Elliot and Van Horne is that they are always looking for the cutting edge of the market and for new niches in the global marketplace to invest. Once the niche grows large, they move on to the next opportunity.

"What drives me, what gets me excited, what gets my juices flowing is finding the new opportunity, finding the new niche where there is an excess return to be earned because a lot of people have not necessarily understood the opportunity that exists," Elliot says.

Van Horne believes that one of the greatest benefits to come out of the carnage of 1998 is Wall Street's lack of desire to pay attention to the emerging markets.

"One of the hallmarks of emerging markets from years ago was lack of information and inefficiencies, and in the last few years that has not been the case since many people have discovered the opportunities of these investments," he says. "I think that we will be getting back to those types of situations because there are not going to be as many people paying attention to what is going on.

"There will be some interesting things to do; the value of traveling around and doing your own research will I think come to the forefront again," he continues. "A lot of the brokerage firms that provided equity reports on Brazil and other emerging markets are not going to be doing it anymore. To the extent that there are two or three guys looking at a bank in Brazil instead of ten guys, there most likely will be much greater investment opportunity."

Although technology and information are making the world a smaller, more efficient place in which to get market data, both Elliot and Van Horne believe that they will always be able to find emerging markets in which to invest successfully.

"I have been managing money since 1980 and I spent my first three years trading foreign exchange, and since then I have always had the same idea in my head, that once you make money in something, you sort of say, 'What is the next opportunity?' " Elliot says. "What we try to do at Croesus is try to increase the odds of finding those opportunities by segmenting the market and having different teams work on different things and then culling those ideas. There are always opportunities in the world as long as you look for them."

Elliot says that in order to be successful you need to be able to adjust your skill set to the market.

"The guys who made money at one phase of the market are not necessarily the guys who make money at a later phase. There is always a sweet spot," he says. "There are always guys who are in the sweet spot and often people mistake those guys for geniuses because they made good returns. But the reality is that maybe they had the right skills, maybe they were in the right place at the right time, or maybe they were most leveraged—but the market moves on.

"We know that we will never be in all of the sweet spots or that we will be the first ones in, but we do know that if we are mature, sophisticated people, we will be able to produce a nice return over time," he continues. "There will always be someone who gets a little more juice out of something, but we believe we will be able to be consistent."

Van Horne thinks that people sometimes lose sight of what investing in emerging markets is all about—a theory that both he and Elliot quote quite frequently—the difference between perception and reality.

"One way to think about investing in emerging markets is to look at the difference between perception and reality; and the ideal investment opportunity to discover is the one where the market is pricing an asset based on its perception, and the perception is far removed from reality," Van Horne says. "By doing research and by applying ourselves and experience coupled with the special expertise of the people we are partnering with, we can develop a view of what the reality is; and to the extent that we develop a very high level of conviction that we have done our work and we are right about what the reality is, then we put our money into it and eventually perception comes our way if we are right, and the market pricing follows."

Van Horne believes that places like Brazil, Russia, and Croatia all exemplify the divergence between perception and reality.

"It is not that perception is untrue—that there is not corruption and Mafia-type influence—but you do not make money on the perception," he says. "You make money on reality, so there is some truth to perception but the real truth is where the reality is and that is where money is made."

At the end of 1997, the main fund was up 31 percent and had annual compounded return since inception of approximately 39 percent. The fund is accepting new money and has had steady inflows over the past few years. Because of the nature of its investments, it has found that its approach has allowed it to stay hot while other funds have fallen out of favor.

"Our ability to offer investors interesting things other than straight run-of-the-mill emerging market investment opportunities allows us to market our business successfully," Van Horne says. "We think our investment style is interesting because we are looking for themes that should make money and because we have some of the best people in the world working on putting our strategies in place."

One thing making it more challenging for Croesus is that a lot more brokers and investment banks and managers are trying to do what it is doing. In the past few years there has been an explosion of emerging market funds, and Croesus has had to adapt to the idea that it has to continue to find good investment opportunities in places where there is more competition.

"The way to continue to provide valuable services to the clients—and that valuable service is good risk-reward mix and good investment returns—is to do what we are doing, which is to find opportunities that provide a return that is outsized by the risk we are taking," Van Horne says. "I am convinced that these opportunities will remain there for at least 15 years, and what we need to do is to make sure that we keep focusing and we go deeper into these areas that we are focusing on."

By forming partnerships with people where the firm believes opportunities exist, Croesus believes it can capture returns that others cannot.

"We are constantly looking for new opportunities, and what we have had to do more and more is be sensitive to the world macro situation," Van Horne says. "As fundamentals change around the globe, we need to pay attention to liquidity issues and global flows of money because it will impact the prices of stocks in emerging markets as much as a country's political or social climate, as such things have gotten more complicated since we started the fund."

Van Horne believes that the fund can grow to twice its size and produce solid returns because the markets continue to develop.

At the time of our meeting Elliot was focusing on researching and exploring opportunities in Africa. Croesus established a fund to invest in Africa that looked at four types of plays on the continent and in its developing nations. Croesus invests in current and noncurrent African debt, provides seed financing to new ventures, and makes equity investments.

"There are always countries going down while some are going up, so there may not be an after-Africa place for us," Elliot says. "For example, people always say that the Ukraine is three years behind Russia, but the Ukraine is heading south and it is seven years behind Russia. So maybe in three years' time, when it's 15 years behind Russia, it will become interesting. If you look at the real opportunity and segment it, that is where you can get the excess return."

DALE JACOBS

Dale Jacobs believes he is unique when it comes to today's hedge fund managers. Not only does he operate a fund that invests solely in stocks in the financial services industry, but he also employs the classic Jones model of hedge fund management: He uses shorts to manage risk.

Jacobs, who is in his mid-fifties, is president and portfolio manager of Financial Investors Inc., a fund he started in 1992 after working for 25 years at a number of Wall Street's premier firms. The fund is up over 430 percent since inception, besting the S&P by over 200 points and the Keefe, Bruyette and Woods Inc. bank stock index by over 150 points. Like most funds, however, it found that 1998 was not a good year and the fund did post a loss at year-end.

"We have been able to put up the performance numbers by doing what we say we were going to do in our offering memo," he says. "By sticking to our plan, working hard, and understanding that not every stock pick is going to be a home run, we have been able to be consistent over time, a trend we think will continue."

Although many may think of Jacobs as operating a sector fund—meaning the fund invests solely in one industry and its performance rests on how well the industry performs—he does not believe that is what he does.

"I don't regard us a classical sector fund, because as a hedge fund we bring a lot more to the table," he says. "If we truly operate as a hedge fund, meaning that we are hedged, that we are opportunistic, and that we can make money in both negative and positive markets, this is a whole different type of investment strategy applied to the sector and as such comparing us to a mutual fund that invests in the financial services community is like comparing apples to oranges.

"Investing in a mutual fund sector fund is just a 100 percent bet

117

on whatever the sector is that they are investing in," he continues. "While we are 100 percent exposed to the sector, we are not 100 percent exposed to the performance of the sector because of the strategy, philosophy, and discipline that we follow."

Jacobs believes that it is very hard for investors truly to understand that definition, but he believes that it is critical to understanding the way he operates his fund.

"If a sector fund set up as a hedge fund is only long, well then that is a mutual fund disguised as a hedge fund which is charging hedge fund fees, and that is wrong," he says. "The concept of a hedge fund is to employ hedging, and in today's environment not many people are following the concept.

"Our job to reduce risk and to reduce volatility while being able to employ all the tools available to us as investment managers to outperform the market," he continues. "If a hedge fund does not do that, then what is the investor paying for? The manager is not reducing risk and in some cases may be taking on more risk through leverage—and that is not what a hedge fund is supposed to be doing."

Jacobs believes that many "small behind-the-scenes" managers who are not well known are following a strict investment process that allows them to reduce risk while putting up good returns. He considers himself in this category.

"Our job is to minimize risk while maximizing returns and the only way we know how to do it is by following a strict investment philosophy that does not use leverage to outperform the market," he says. "We have a definite view on the market and through fundamental analysis we are able to use whatever tools necessary to be successful."

Jacobs develops his ideas on the market as well as the economy from a number of sources. Besides reading everything he can get his hands on and listening to various people, he also works closely with Dr. Beryl L. Sprinkle, who was President Reagan's under secretary of the Treasury and chairman of the Council of Economic Advisers.

"His job is to help me formulate a macro view of the economy and the Federal Reserve interest rate policy," Jacobs says. "Sprinkle is the starting point for where our macro view comes from and we sort of fill in the blanks by installing the information we get from being alert.

"I am less knowledgeable about the overall market valuation consideration issues than I am about the overall market for bank and thrift stocks valuation, and yet one is clearly tied to another," he continues. "By working with him we are able to really understand interest rates and Federal Reserve policy and what that means, and then I extrapolate what that means for the banking industry and bank stock prices."

And what a time to be focusing on banking and thrift stocks. Over the past nine years, the industry has been in constant flux, from steady impact of deregulation to the creation of national and super-regional banking behemoths. Throughout it all, Jacobs has had his finger on the pulse of the industry, finding unique investment and trading opportunities.

"We are in an excellent period of attractive valuations and that has been the case since 1991; the case to own financial stocks—in particular, the case to own banks and thrifts—is a very strong case," he says. "Some people would look at multiples and say these multiples are sky-high and not justified, and I don't agree. They are high only if you compare them to historic valuations of absolute price-to-earnings ratios. But on a relative basis they are not high, and they continue to be at a discount to the overall S&P."

Jacobs believes that valuation is just one reason to own this group of stocks. "Any industry that is consolidating is a good one to invest in," he says.

Although consolidation has ebbed and flowed since the 1980s, Jacobs believes that it will continue for many years.

"The BankAmerica-NationsBank merger creates the largest domestic bank in the country and it only has about 10 percent of the deposits in the country. There is no other country in the world where you have a bank that has 10 percent and nobody else is close to it," he says. "There is huge room for consolidation and it will go on for a long time to come."

The third reason Jacobs believes the banking industry is attractive is because of its very active capital management.

"Until only recently, the banking industries' management was guided by the concept of preservation of capital. No one ever wanted to buy stock back," he says. "Now the banks are generating so much earnings that they cannot use in their business that we see capital levels growing tremendously. So the issues to management are how do we use this capital in the most effective way for shareholder returns? And as such they are doing different things like buying back stock or making purchase accounting acquisitions, and now they are doing more that will employ cash as part of the compensation."

Jacobs also believes that management has taken a turn for the better. As consolidation continues, he says, managers are much more attuned to efficiency and understanding the cost of doing business.

"One of the motivating factors in the acquisition boom is to put two organizations together, either through a merger of equals or just an outright acquisition, where you can take cost out of the combined company," he says.

Another factor that makes the financial services industry attractive to Jacobs is its ability to develop new products and new distribution channels. The ability to sell insurance and other products and services, combined with the ability to distribute services through automated teller machines and supermarket branches, has created a good environment for shareholders, because revenue flows right to the bottom line.

"There are a number of different themes that are going on in the industry. When you overlay on top of it the fact that these companies are operating and producing returns that are far higher than the S&P 500 returns, and you put all this stuff together and ask how could it be that they sell at a discount to the S&P? The answer is they shouldn't," he says. "I can't tell you why they do other than to say that historically that has been the case, and maybe a lot of portfolio managers are still dealing with their historic understanding of why and how bank stocks should be valued."

Technology also makes banks attractive. "Technology is changing the way you define what a bank is and how it operates," he points out. "A bank can operate solely on the Internet. If the bank can make the connection to its customers friendly, easy, and appropriate for all the services it wants to sell, then it can really change the direction of the industry faster than ever was imaginable."

To stay on top of the industry, Jacobs is in constant contact with management. "A common view of people who don't necessarily invest in banks and are just users of bank services may be that a bank is a bank is a bank, but there is nothing further from the truth," he says. "Every bank believes that it has a unique strategy that differentiates itself from the next institution, and investors don't always see these differences and can't appreciate how one franchise is different from each other. Citibank is one type of institution; Northern Trust in Chicago is another. They are totally different but they are both banks. They are unique and think of as well as manage themselves differently from each other, and this is very exciting for my business."

Jacobs operates his fund using three major components. One is a group of investments in money-center and large regional bank stocks, ranging between 20 percent of the portfolio and zero, depending on the situation in the market. At the other end of the portfolio, he buys small community and niche-oriented bank and thrift stocks that are thinly traded. These positions are not very liquid and usually consist of 20 percent of the portfolio. The remaining assets—the bulk of the portfolio—are in everything in between: banks and thrifts of good size anywhere in the country (the fund holds no foreign stocks or private placement investments). He uses fundamental analysis to guide him in acquiring and trading these stocks.

In most cases, Jacobs does not own a position for more than a year because something usually happens to suggest that he has maximized value or, on the other hand, the stock hasn't performed well.

"We are not just buying a stock and looking at it on its own. We look at it in relation to what else we can invest in and determine if the stock is a really good buy and why we should be buying it," he says. "Every day we think, should we continue to own, should we buy more, or should we sell it, so we are constantly thinking about and determining what we should do about positions."

When Jacobs is fully invested, the fund may have 90 stocks in its portfolio. The day we met, it had just 60 stocks. At times when things look uncertain or negative, and yet the fundamentals for the group are good—meaning that business is good and earnings are on target—he won't short. Instead, he will be less long to raise cash. Still, in a market like 1990's, with a major sell-off because of real estate worries, dwindling capital, and a huge number of nonperforming loans, Jacobs finds fundamental reasons to short the group, because he knows he can make money on the downside.

"One of the classic things that has been advantageous for us is if you say, 'I don't want to own this stock,' and if you say that then you should short it," he asserts. "The mutual fund manager says, 'I don't want to own it; let's raise cash,' while the true hedge fund manager says, 'I don't want to own it; I want to short it. I want to make money going down.' "

Jacobs hedges his portfolio using both short positions and index puts; that is, various options on a specific index that protect the portfolio should things go south.

Financial Investors Inc. consists of an offshore fund, a domestic partnership, and a few small secondary partnerships, Jacobs would not disclose the amount of assets under management.

"Size does not motivate me; performance motivates me," he says. "We have been doing very well over time and we have compounded net to the investor in excess of 20 percent for the past seven years, and that is what I would like to continue doing.

"It is not a business where you say, 'Let's put in a few extra hours and we can get some performance.' It just does not work that way," he continues. "I firmly believe that in the money management business, you have to have a philosophy, a discipline, and an approach that you stay with over time. The key to being successful is the ability to change or to adapt the approach based on market conditions, not on performance."

GUY WYSER-PRATTE

Unlike other hedge fund managers who operate in obscurity and seem only to cater to their high-net-worth clients, Guy Wyser-Pratte is truly

a man of the people. His fund and the firm that bears his name specialize in risk arbitrage and corporate governance.

Wyser-Pratte has been working on Wall Street for more than 25
years and is often called the dean of the arbitrage community. In the
past few years, however, his efforts to champion shareholder rights and
to change many aspects of corporate governance strategies have won
him many headlines as well as earning his investors superior returns.

"Our efforts to change the framework of corporate governance in
the United States will destroy the 'just-say-no' defense that so many
companies try to use when they are faced with a threat to their auton-
omy," he says. "It will end the abuses of *poison pill* and will force boards
to think and act in the best interest of shareholders, something they often overlook.

poison pill   any number of legal defensive tactics
written into a corporate charter to fend off the
advances of an unwanted suitor.

"People are fed up with the way management has been using poison pills. Instead of using them as tools to protect the company and its
shareholders, management has been using poison pills as tools for en-
trenchment," he continued.

The poison pill was invented in the 1980s to give management
significant control over the success or failure of a hostile takeover bid.
Poison pills give shareholders the right to purchase hundreds of millions of dollars worth of shares very cheaply, which in turn often scares
the suitor off because of the significantly increased number of shares
needed to gain control.

Wyser-Pratte believes that instead of benefiting the shareholder,
the use of poison pills often harms them, because bidders aware of the
pills' existence will not attempt a takeover. This keeps shareholders
from realizing the maximum value of their investment and allows

management to keep power. Therefore, he has designed the "chewable poison pill."

He says, "Our pill keeps the best aspects of the conventional poison pill but at the same time it does not allow management to entrench themselves. It forces management to act in the best interests of shareholders at all times."

The first example of the chewable poison pill's use came in late 1997, when Union Pacific Resources Inc. withdrew its unfriendly bid to take over Pennzoil Corp. Union Pacific had offered $84 a share for Pennzoil, but the oil company threw up a just-say-no defense. The unsolicited bid offered a $20-a-share premium and would have added $1 billion to the company's market capitalization. Once Union Pacific pulled out, however, Wyser-Pratte stepped in, figuring that there was no basis for management's turning the deal away. On July 30, 1998, Pennzoil stock was trading in the low $40 range. In late 1997, the stock had been trading in the mid $60s.

Wyser-Pratte forced the company to act in the best interests of shareholders—he was one, since his fund owned over 1.5 percent of Pennzoil—by merging one of its units. It also has adopted a modified poison pill that gives shareholders a voice in future takeover offers. The chewable pill that Pennzoil adopted, based on Wyser-Pratte's efforts, says that if an unsolicited offer comes in at 35 percent over the average trading price, management must take it.

To make the board listen to his ideas, Wyser-Pratte launched a proxy fight, ran for a board seat, and filed a federal lawsuit to change a bylaw regarding board elections. Both sides in early 1998 reached a settlement that included Pennzoil's adding an outside director to its board and adopting a bylaw that gives shareholders the right to call a special meeting outside the annual meeting.

As part of the settlement, Wyser-Pratte dropped his lawsuit and his efforts to become a board member. Wyser-Pratte does not believe it will be the last time he will be able to get a company to adopt his chewable pill.

He has since moved on to fighting the poison pills and their protectors in general instead of in individual companies. As a Marine, he learned about fighting and more importantly about winning.

"This is going to be a battleground of major proportions between us and Delaware and all companies incorporated in Delaware,
because we are going to take this and we are going to be actively as-
sisted by the State of Wisconsin pension board and the Council of Institutional Investors," he says. "We want to have all companies
whose poison pills expire next year adopt the same formula. Shareholders are fed up with the just-say-no defense because they have
lost a lot of money."

Wyser-Pratte believes that his effort to change corporate governance is doing what is right by the shareholders. This sentiment is not
often echoed in the hedge fund community. In most cases, hedge fund
operators choose to do good things only after they have made their
fortunes and can devote time to charitable organizations. Wyser-
Pratte, on the other hand, makes it part of his everyday money management duties.

"When management hides behind their poison pill, they undo
whatever amount of corporate democracy exists and make a mockery
out of corporate governance," he argues.

He became interested in corporate governance issues when he was
running Prudential Bache's arbitrage group. In 1974, he owned preferred stock in the sugar company Great Western United, but when the
time came to receive his dividends, he realized something was amiss.
Sugar prices were surging, but the checks never arrived. Finally, he and
a colleague decided to sue the company for the dividends they were
owed. Within a matter of days of the filing of the suit, a check arrived
from the company and he realized that he could make money by becoming a shareholder activist.

Before 1974, he had been an arbitrageur. Arbitrage—in its most
simple definition—is the buying of an article in one market and selling
it in another. He learned the business of equity arbitrage from his father, who started the Wyser-Pratte firm in 1929 in Paris. It was subsequently merged into Bache & Co. and then into Prudential. In 1990,
Wyser-Pratte resurrected the firm as a stand-alone entity—severing his
ties with Prudential and operating the firm independently as his father
had before him.

Wyser-Pratte usually works on three or four deals at a time, some in the United States and some in Europe.

"We try to focus on the best opportunities and work very hard at making them work for us instead of working on as many deals as possible," he says. "The way we determine what is worth doing is by looking at the amount of risk we have to take compared to the rate of return we expect from taking the risk. Something with a low return with a high risk is something we would avoid while something with a high return with low risk is something we would be very interested in working on."

Another situation that Wyser-Pratte was involved with was Tattinger S.A., the French hotel and champagne conglomerate, of which he and his partners control approximately 13 percent of the stock.

"We keep accumulating the stock and telling management that they have got to do what is right for shareholders. We are drawing attention to the undervalued assets in the company," he says. "Over there what we are doing is admired by the shareholder population, but the establishment hates our guts."

The fund's efforts to increase shareholder value in Tattinger S.A. were the subject of a front-page article in *The Wall Street Journal* on November 11, 1998.

Wyser-Pratte usually gets involved when a buyer walks away from a deal because the company has refused to accept the offer that is on the table. Once he gets involved, he works to make the deal happen. Although he does not talk to the suitor or have any kind of agreement with the company, his efforts are always focused on maximizing value for shareholders—which usually include him.

"In most cases when a buyer walks away from a deal, they are expecting us to get involved, to run the company up a yardarm somewhere," he says. "Most suitors know that if we think the company is not acting in the best interest of the shareholder, we will turn our guns on them and make them maximize shareholder value."

There have been a number of times when Wyser-Pratte has heard of a situation and for whatever reason decided to get involved not by purchasing stock but strictly as an activist. Two cases of this were with the American International Group's attempt to buy American Bankers

Insurance without letting others bid on it and Echlin Inc.'s attempt to get an antishareholder law passed in Connecticut. In both cases, his funds owned stock in the companies but Wyser-Pratte felt that he needed to take action to force the companies to look out for their shareholders.

"When you see that you can actually get things done by having the force of conviction to actually do something, that makes it fun," he says.

The firm's funds have grown quite successful. Wyser-Pratte launched them with less than $5 million under management and at year-end 1997 had over $600 million. Since 1967, he has posted annual compounded returns of 29.78 percent, while the Standard & Poor's 500 stock index returned just 13.34 percent for the same period. Prior to launching the fund, Wyser-Pratte managed money at Prudential Bache. His performance record includes all of the years for which he managed money both in and outside of Prudential.

His firm operates out of lower Manhattan with 12 individuals. For the most part, he makes all investment decisions and works with colleagues to implement his strategies. Since the firm has been independent, Wyser-Pratte has done over 15 corporate governance deals, both in the United States and in Europe, and all have been successful. His investors are both high-net-worth individuals and pension funds.

Wyser-Pratte's efforts in corporate governance have come from paying close attention to what goes on in Europe.

"Our experience operating overseas has taught us how to work around a lot of the issues we are faced with here in the United States," he says. "Overseas, they don't have this nonsense. The key idea over there is to protect shareholders, not to entrench management. Here, because of the American Bar Association, the whole thing is to perpetuate litigation around the poison pill, and all they are doing is wasting shareholder money."

Born in Vichy, France, in 1940, he moved to the United States with his family in 1947 and became a U.S. citizen in 1953. Wyser-Pratte was graduated from New York University with an MBA. The Marine Corps discharged him as a captain in 1966. He learned arbitrage from his father, Eugene Wyser-Pratte, who practiced the classical arbitrage strategy of buying stocks in one market and selling them in another.

"I did not find his business interesting at all," Wyser-Pratte recalls. "He explained to me that the business was getting more interesting and more intellectually challenging, so I decided to give it a look."

In 1967, his father decided to merge the family firm into Bache & Co. to have access to a larger pool of capital. He stayed with the firm until retiring in January 1971.

Guy Wyser-Pratte took over the unit and eventually came to run all of Prudential Bache's arbitrage activities. The situation got contentious in the late 1980s and early 1990s when Prudential was reeling from its limited partnership problems. When he was told that the firm had no more capital to use for proprietary trading because the securities firm's parent, Prudential Insurance Company of America, had shut it off, he decided to leave in 1991.

"In 1992, I did a lot of road shows and all I could raise was $3 million," he remembers. "But since then we have grown to our current size, and in six years I think we are doing very well. There is nothing quite like running your own show and it is particularly helpful with all we do in corporate governance because we don't have to ask before we go after a company."

Asking proved to be a problem when he was working at Prudential Bache. Wyser-Pratte sued Houston Natural Gas because the board had turned down a bid and had prevented a subsequent bid from coming into the boardroom. He cleared the suit right to the top of Prudential after explaining that the firm's interests had been damaged. No one checked with the president, however, who happened to be in the office of the chairman of Houston Natural Gas at the minute the news flashed on the tape saying "Pru-Bache files suit against Houston Natural Gas."

"The chairman was about to sign a huge investment banking deal with Prudential and needless to say it did not get signed," he says. "Eventually, the chairman of Houston Natural Gas was fired for his actions and another firm emerged to take over the company."

Wyser-Pratte believes that his training in the Marine Corps is the most formative experience he has ever had and that it has played a significant part in his ability to succeed in business: "Being a Marine has helped me tremendously on Wall Street in building my career. It taught me how to size people up when I am in a situation where character is called upon. You can judge pretty quickly who you can count on and who you can't when there is danger, and that skill is very important to being successful on Wall Street."

Although Wyser-Pratte has a lot of fun pursuing corporate governance situations, he is still very focused on exploiting arbitrage opportunities. As an arbitrageur, Wyser-Pratte gets involved with stocks when companies announce a deal. His method is to try to profit by capturing the spread between the price of the stock of the acquirer and that of the acquired.

"As long as we keep our discipline and do not go crazy in one situation while going about our business methodically we will be successful," he affirms.

Wyser-Pratte springs into action when a prospective deal is announced. Immediately following the announcement he and his team evaluate it and try to determine if it makes business sense. If they find that the risks and potential returns seem worthwhile, they invest.

Although corporate governance is where Wyser-Pratte gets all of the headlines, the firm still uses classical arbitrage strategies to post returns for its investors. He uses his risk arbitrage skills to determine the likelihood of the success of mergers and acquisitions, and usually when a deal takes place his firm has a position in the companies' stock.

"The key to being successful in this business is to continue to get better at what we are trying to do," he says. "We need to stay focused on strategies that we know will work and build our skills around those strategies."

In the Pennzoil situation, Wyser-Pratte was able to use both his corporate governance and his arbitrage skills to achieve a solid return. The oil company basically was fed up with fighting him and decided that the best solution would be to settle. As part of the settlement, the company agreed to his proposed bylaw and added an independent director to its board.

"It was a win-win situation for both of us," he says. "They were able to get what they wanted and I got what I wanted—and the shareholders were able to profit."

Once the settlement was reached, Pennzoil decided to merge its motor oil division with Quaker State and spin it off, leaving just the oil exploration company. The spin-off provides Pennzoil shareholders with stock in both entities. Wyser-Pratte believes that once the spin-off is complete, Pennzoil will again be the target of a takeover since the companies that went after Pennzoil in first place would have sold the motor oil division, anyway.

"What is left is an entity that is attractive because it has both a solid business and our chewable poison pill. My guess is that it won't be out there for more than a month before it is bid on," he declares.

At the time we met, Wyser-Pratte owned over a million shares of Pennzoil and planned on selling his interest in the new company and holding on to his shares in the oil exploration company.

Wyser-Pratte believes that there are more important things in life than just lining both his and his investors' pockets.

"I am not involved with philanthropy in my business; my job is to make a decent return for investors," he says. "However, all of us in life look for some moral dimension in what we do, and I am able to fulfill that in what I do for a living."

F. MARTIN KOENIG

Martin Koenig likes things nice and easy. He is not interested in wild market swings and does not want to make a killing one day only to take a hit the next. Koenig likes to be neutral—market neutral, that is.

Koenig is a pure technician.

Unlike many fund managers who use a combination of technical and fundamental research to find investment opportunities, he relies on strategies and theories. His basic belief is that by using *portfolio diversification theory,* he will be able continually to beat the indexes without taking the risk that most fund managers use to post the same type of returns.

> **portfolio diversification theory** the theory assumes that investors want the least possible dispersion of returns for a given level of gain.

The basis for his operation, portfolio diversification theory, says that diversification can be achieved by investing in assets that experience inverse fluctuations in value. In English, when one asset goes up, the other goes down, and by investing in both you will outperform an investment in a single asset.

"On a long-term basis, if you put half your money in gold and half your money in bonds, you will probably get very similar returns based on economic and market factors," he says. "Most people will say, well, if I am going to get a 10 percent return on each, it does not matter if you put half your money in both or put all of it one. When you look at return it may be true, but when you look risk it is wrong."

While gold and bonds may have the same *volatility* risk, Koenig is quick to point out that because the price fluctuations are out of phase with each other, you are able to reduce your total portfolio volatility if you put half in one and half in the other.

> **volatility** the degree of fluctuation over a given period in a security based on the standard deviation of the price.

"You end up with the same compounded rate of return but because the assets move in opposite directions your return is much more stable," he points out. "Return per unit of risk improves while you are able to also decrease the amount of volatility in the portfolio."

Koenig also uses portfolio rebalancing to make sure that each time the assets move he is able to take out excess growth from the portfolio.

"As long as the two asset classes tend to be mean reverted, which means that they get to extremes and then move back toward the norm, rebalancing will work," he says. "Basically, it means that at the end of a period you end up with a return that is actually higher than the return of each one of the asset classes by themselves, averaged."

Koenig believes the process reduces risk and also increases the expected return a modest amount.

"You need to invest in asset styles and classes that are not correlated with one another," he says. "Not only do you know that you are going to reduce your risk, but you also know that you are likely to get a return that is slightly higher than the arithmetic averages of all the styles, strategies, and asset classes that you are using. If you do that, it is much better than investing in one style because your return per unit of risk is vastly improved. The key is to maximize your return per unit of risk."

Koenig uses a number of other measures to evaluate investment opportunities. One is *drawdowns*. He tries to determine what the worst case could be for the portfolio in time periods ranging from quarters and months to weeks and days.

draw down   percentage of loss during a given period.

"You need to be able to minimize both the size and the frequency of drawdowns because they can be particularly dangerous if you are leveraged," he advises. "We like to skew our return patterns so that our upside volatility is greater than our downside volatility, and that is not easy to do. But by doing so, we are able to measure risk and act accordingly to limit our exposure to risk."

He does not believe that one ratio or risk-return measure is absolute. However, he does think the most important thing to do when constructing a portfolio is to base it on two important principles: to minimize risk and to maximize the rate of return.

"If you focus on maximizing return and don't pay any attention to risk, you are going to blow up," he says.

At the time we met in the Spring of 1998, Koenig thought the overall market was overpriced. The portfolios consisted of positions that included being short large-cap stocks and long mid- and small-cap stocks.

"For the most part, we keep our portfolios in balance because it is a very risky game to play," he says. "But when you see certain things fall into place, the risk subsides, and it is at that point that we tilt the portfolio."

Koenig is obsessed with getting rid of general market risk. To do this he constructs various portfolios that are mirror images of the trends he is following. For example, he will construct a portfolio that consists of contrarian, overvalued, and trend-following poor-growth stocks, which are the antithesis of his existing long portfolios. So if he puts the two together he ends up with a portfolio that is long 10 million and short 10 million, and hopefully he is generating returns that consist of higher numbers while keeping risk in check.

"If we are outperforming on our longs and underperforming on our shorts, we are able to take advantage of the lower volatility and the diversity that each of them offers," he says. "Each will go in opposite directions on a chart, which keeps the portfolio stable with the bottom line being that the overall portfolio will outperform the market by 200 to 300 basis points while not increasing risk at all."

Some people have looked at what Koenig does and call it nothing more than "an enhanced return Treasury bill strategy." That means it has close to zero volatility with a somewhat higher standard deviation risk that provides an expected return of approximately double Treasury bills.

"I am able to earn 5 percent on my cash for short sale proceeds, and I get another 5 percent on stock selection, which gives me a 10 percent return," he says. "But, in some respects when you look at the volatility characteristics as measured by beta, I have something very similar to a Treasury bill."

Koenig's investors like his style because there are not many places where you can get double Treasury bill returns while maintaining the same risk parameters.

"We do have a little bit more volatility than T-bills, but we are getting double returns with it and it is very attractive," he says.

For most people that would be enough, but Koenig is not most people. Therefore he continually tries to improve his returns by "ratcheting the risk down." He explains, "We can try to bring the risk down without hampering our expected rate of return. I don't mind if we drop the risk and drop the return somewhat as long as our return per unit of risk improves or stays the same."

He believes that if he can get the risk level low enough, it is then safe to start using leverage.

"If I can earn double T-bills and I can borrow at 100 basis points over Treasury bills, paying 6 percent for my money, and make 10 percent, all I have to worry about is the risk associated with the trades," he says. "But you need to keep leverage in check, because if you get to 200-to-1 you have a risk of a blowup, but if you go three- or four-to-one, like we are doing, well, then I think it is pretty safe."

Koenig has designed a fund that has three classes of investors. Similar to class A, B, and C shares, New World Partners has three ways for investors to participate. The first class is called Preferred Members. Investors get a piece of floating-rate paper that initially pays 100 basis points over the Treasury-bill rate and comes with a potential for being 35 percent tax free for corporate investors. Koenig believes he can achieve this tax status because half of the returns that go to the investor will come in the form of qualified dividends. Although Koenig was not marketing this class of shares in the fund when we met, he was planning to roll it out to defined benefit plans.

"This is a way for defined benefit plans to actually use leverage that is not debt and has no interest cost. It is perfectly permissible un-der ERISA [Employee Retirement Income Security Act] and it has no unrelated business taxable income problems," he says. "When pen-sion plans invest in a leveraged fund with interest cost, they are going to lose some of their tax-free status. In this case it is a preferred par-ticipation certificate and they will not lose any of their tax status. It is a nice little tax arbitrage for both corporate and defined benefit plan investors."

New World offers a second class of shares to investors who are called Members. In this class, Koenig assures investors that 90 percent of their capital is protected and that the investments are unleveraged.

The third class, Subordinated Members, uses three-to-one lever-age. Investors are protected up to 66 percent of their capital.

"Investors know up front what the worst-case scenario is in the event that we blow up, because of the stop loss provisions in each of the classes," he says. "If you take the floating paper you are not going to lose anything, if you are unleveraged you may lose 10 cents on the dol-lar, and if you are leveraged you may lose a third of your money. There is no other leveraged hedge fund that I know of that tells investors what they will get back if it blows up. We think it is a nice feature that is to-tally unique to us."

Koenig uses very sophisticated stock selection software that he and his partner developed while he was running Chase Manhattan Bank's market-neutral portfolio.

"Basically, the technology rates the entire universe of stocks and places them in a matrix. The system analyzes 15 fundamental factors, as well as future earnings characteristics and other technical informa-tion," he explains.

"The difference between what we do and what most of Wall Street does is that we pick stocks through the use of thoroughly objective models," he says. "Most analysts use models that can be jury-rigged to come up with buy or sell recommendations. If the analysts like the stock, they use data that will cause the number to be positive; if they don't like the stock, they use data that will cause the number to be negative."

One factor that Koenig weighs is all the upward and downward revisions in analysts' earnings estimates. Say, for example, that 15 analysts cover a stock. If 10 revise estimates upward while the others issue downward revisions, the system subtracts the reduced estimates from the increased estimates and then divides that number by the total number of analysts. That produces a score in which the highest-ranked stock is considered the best investment.

Besides using his own system to handle the quantitative long-short/short-market neutral and hedging overlay strategies, Koenig also uses a number of other noncorrelating styles and strategies to manage the portfolio. They include global risk arbitrage, global convertible arbitrage, value equity management, mean reversion statistical arbitrage, and deep hidden value. For these styles and strategies, Koenig relies on a variety of managers whom he has worked with for many years as subadvisers. None of the subadvisers have discretion over any part of the fund. Their only role is to provide research and information.

To determine the strengths of his subadvisers, Koenig took all their numbers along with his own and put them together to see how the portfolio would have done over the past nine years.

"By using pro formas that contain actual numbers," he says, "we can see what happened in the past and then all we have to do is mix and match managers to see who fits with our strategies. It is completely different than what commodities guys do when they test their theories and try to come up with what they believe is a new way to predict the future."

He continues, "All they really are doing is finding a new way to fit performance to a method by using data and there is no assurance it will work in the future. What we use are actual numbers of actual managers to perform various tests to determine what styles and strategies will and will not work."

Koenig believes that a lot of managers who think they have found a new way to forecast the market are really just fooling themselves and investors, and are likely to blow up.

"If you divide the history into two different time periods," he says, "and you do your research on one time period without any knowledge of what the other time period looks like, and then you use the same mix in the other time period and you get similar characteristics, you have probably found something of value. You know it may work because you have not data-mined, you have not over-fitted the line, and you have not fooled yourself, and you will not fool investors."

The use of multiple styles and strategies from a number of subadvisers allows Koenig to have return streams that do not correlate with one another. Still, for the system to work, the subadvisers make sense and fit into the overall strategy of the fund.

One of the interesting points to the subadviser relationship is that Koenig tested various weighting strategies. In each case—whether it was 60–40, 70–30, or 80–20—he found that the strategies were "amazingly similar and stable" regardless of how they were weighted in the portfolio.

"We line all of the subadvisers up and determine their process. If the process is not clearly understood, we will not touch them," he says. "But, if we understand the process, if we are convinced that the return streams do not correlate with the others, and if the numbers add up, we will consider using them."

When we met, Koenig had $27 million in assets under management in his fund while his registered investment adviser business had over $100 million. He says he would like to see the fund grow to $100 million by the end of 1999 and believes that his style will allow him to manage an infinite amount.

"We feel very confident that what we have will continue to work in the future as long as we continue to follow the same methodology," he says. "The key to our continued success is that we are so structured that even if one piece of the portfolio blows up, we will not blow up."

Koenig believes his own business success comes from his experience working for a Japanese institution early in his career. It was there that he learned to keep trying to make things better regardless of how well something is working.

"They taught me that you can always improve and make what

you have better," he says. "There are two schools of management: the if-it-ain't-broke-don't-fix-it school and the if-you-are-standing-still-you-are-probably-losing-ground school. While it sounds like the two are not compatible, they are and we are trying to do them both at all times."

BILL MICHAELCHECK

On Wall Street, there are stock guys and bond guys.

The stock guys can name all 30 Dow Jones Industrial Average stocks and at what level they opened and closed. The bond guys hang on Alan Greenspan and the Fed's every word and laugh when the popular press reminds their readers and viewers that yield moves in the opposite direction of price.

I am a bond guy. All of my formal Wall Street training was at a bond house and I still make the bulk of my living trading and selling U.S. Treasuries.

So naturally, when I saw Bill Michaelcheck on one of the cable news channels talking about the Treasury market and his hedge fund, I became interested in learning more about him and his operation.

Michaelcheck is a bond guy. Since the early 1970s, after earning an MBA at Harvard, he has been trading Treasuries. He spent the early part of his career at J. F. Eckstein and Co. and the World Bank before finding a home at Bear, Stearns & Co. Inc., where he built the Wall Street powerhouse's bond department. Working alongside Wall Street legend Alan "Ace" Greenberg, Michaelcheck created a significant business at Bear, Stearns and, as a partner in the private firm that eventually went public, was rewarded handsomely.

In 1992, Michaelcheck launched Mariner Investment Group, a traditional hedge fund, in order to have a safe vehicle to manage his money. At the time we met in the summer of 1998, the organization had around $300 million under management.

"Over the past few years, our organization has evolved into what I would call a professional manager," he says. "That means we manage money in-house and that we also allocate money to other fund managers."

Mariner currently has two "products" that it uses to manage its partners' money. The firm's original hedge fund is a low-risk vehicle that focuses on U.S. Treasury arbitrage and is managed completely in-house. It also offers a *fund of funds* that is a bit more aggressive that is managed through allocations to outside money managers.

 fund of funds   an investment vehicle that invests in other hedge funds.

The firm also acts as the asset manager for an insurance company of which Michaelcheck is the chairman—a situation very similar to Warren Buffett's role at Berkshire Hathaway Inc.

"Today hedge funds fall into two categories. [The first category is] the Julian Robertson and George Soros people, who are really institutions, that have whole organizations and are really big companies," he says. "Then you have virtually nothing but a few billion-dollar guys, and then you hit the rest of us—people who have anywhere from $10 million to $500 million.

"What we want is to be a conduit for people to manage their money," he continues. "Look, if someone wants to buy Robertson or Soros, they don't need us; but if they want to buy the ocean of other people which includes us, you better know what you are doing because you could really make mistakes."

Michaelcheck believes his organization will succeed because the needs of investors as well as the landscape of the industry have changed dramatically in the past five years.

"It used to be that there was some worldly guy who was a senior partner at some firm, who had $10 million in hedge fund investments with five different friends," he says. "Now you have big family offices and institutions that are putting out hundreds of millions of dollars in

$10 million and $20 million chunks and they don't want to spread it around to guys sitting in their garage in Greenwich smoking cigars. It scares them, because if the manager blows up, the guy loses his job.

"So we are fashioning ourselves as an asset management firm that does hedge funds both internally and externally," he continues. "We are not consultants—we are hands-on managers who have been on the Street and understand that past performance is *not* an indication of future performance."

Michaelcheck thinks he is setting an example because, unlike others who have tried to build similar types of businesses, he and his colleagues were traders and are traders. They are in the markets daily and have been around the markets for a very long time.

"We have created a better mousetrap both internally and externally," he asserts. "We are not trying to be a personality cult. We want the business to be a business and we don't want our income hinging on the health of one of us."

Mariner evolved into its current form after Michaelcheck realized that there was an opportunity to provide to others the service that he needed for his own wealth.

"We are something like a fund of funds and we are a hedge fund," he says. "We are basically something completely unique in the world in which we operate."

At its offices in midtown Manhattan, the company trades fixed-income securities employing various arbitrage strategies in the Treasury and corporate bond markets. The firm also trades technology stocks using stock-versus-warrant arbitrage strategies to capture profits through market movements.

"We primarily run a low-risk hedge fund that takes advantage of price discrepancies in various fixed-income markets," he says. "We are not in this to get our adrenaline up; we are in this to make reasonable returns as risk free as we possibly can. By putting on lots of small trades that allow us to pick up a few basis points here and there, we are able to accomplish this goal."

The money the firm farms out goes to managers whose styles range from high-yield arbitrage and takeover arbitrage to other arbitrage strategies. The difference between what the firm does itself and what it farms out is that the outside managers use "a little higher octane" than do the in-house handlers.

"Having come from the bond world, I do not have much faith in directional equity trading. While things appear to be easy right now, I have not found them to be easy and don't believe in it," he says. "I want to be able to understand what happens and what I think should happen, and do not want to rely on the Dow Jones Industrial Average. I don't need to hit home runs. I am happy employing strategies that have very little risk but allow me to pick up lots of nickels and dimes instead of occasionally picking up dollars."

Michaelcheck finds potential managers to invest with through word of mouth.

"People seem to know what we are doing and give us a call and tell us to check out this person or that person and we look and see if what they are doing fits our investment criteria," he says. "We don't care about how a fund ranks or rates on the various industry databases because it is not how we operate. We know a lot of people who know a lot of people who give us ideas."

The firm looks for fund managers who are employing arbitrage and other market-neutral strategies, as well as those using event-driven business strategies, like takeovers, divestitures, spin-offs, and bankruptcies, things that the managers can thoroughly understand and wrap their hands around. Once Michaelcheck determines which funds to invest in, he performs stress tests on the portfolio and tries to come up with a balanced portfolio of funds that can produce solid returns over various market conditions.

Michaelcheck believes that it is virtually impossible to pick stocks. If you look at all the mutual funds of the world and all their portfolio managers, he believes very few know what they are doing.

"There are always a few exceptions but statistically speaking you are more likely to find diamonds in a mound of coal," he says. "Therefore, if no one can pick stocks, then no one can pick long and short stocks, and most hedge funds are throwing darts at a board.

"Everyone's stockbroker, every mutual fund manager, and almost every hedge fund manager claims to be the one person in the world who can pick stocks, and 99 percent of them cannot," he continues. "Being a hedge fund manager focused solely on stocks is a great marketing tool that is good for business, but for the most part the investors are getting the shaft."

Michaelcheck says that most of the hedge funds in today's marketplace do not add value to investors, and he believes that this is becoming more and more evident when the market moves sideways.

"If you look at the risk-adjusted returns of many hedge funds compared to those of the S&P or Treasuries, you find that very few categories of hedge funds have a positive alpha," he points out. "And most are just chugging along with the market. Chugging along with the market is not worth 1 percent plus 20," he says, alluding to hedge funds' usual management fees. "People are better off in index funds."

He continues, "Most of the hedge funds today earn money, good money, but they have a tremendous amount of volatility, and as such the investor would be better off leveraging up the S&P. But, if you look at what we do or others like us, we have volatility that is less than the five-year Treasury and are able to sustain reasonable growth no matter what the market situation."

That being the case, Mariner does not always sail along smoothly. In July and August of 1998 Mariner's fund hit rough seas and lost money for the first time since its inception. Prior to that period, the fund had never had a down month.

Michaelcheck believes it was the result of the chaos in the bond market during the summer.

"The summer was a disaster," he says. "At the time, the debt market was forecasting a recession, junk bonds had widened to the highest spread in five years, and high-grade corporate bonds had widened because people had really started to worry that there was going to be a credit crunch."

When we met, Mariner was invested in 20-some hedge funds and the net total return for July 1998 was 14 basis points. (A basis point is one hundredth of a percentage point.)

"These are brilliant investment managers, but with all the ups and downs, the only guys making money are the hedge fund guys, because they are able to get 1 percent of total assets," he says. "Meanwhile, we are left waiting for them to do something for us."

Michaelcheck thinks that current market conditions are eerily similar to the situation 30 years ago when hedge funds took it on the chin and a number of funds blew up and went out of business.

"Right now, you can make a strong case that we are in the type of situation that we had in 1968. The market shot up, everyone on the Street started a hedge fund, and then a lot blew up," he says. "My own opinion is that managers will not be able to keep posting the level of returns that investors have become accustomed to, and although we will not have a crash, many of the funds will go out of business because people are not going pay for mediocre returns.

"Stock hedge funds are going to be the first to fall out of favor because managers will not be able to put up 20 percent returns without taking enormous amounts of risk," he continues. "Customers will pull money like they did in 1968 and the industry will take a number of steps backward."

Michaelcheck believes that much of the market turmoil of the summer of 1998 related to the Asian crisis, which set off the Russian crisis, putting fear in U.S. bondholders that a recession was around the corner.

"A lot of people lost a lot of money when Russia got killed," he says. "Many people needed to raise cash for liquidations or to meet margin calls, and to do this they had to sell positions in other stocks because all of the liquidity in the Russian and Asian markets had dried up. You could not sell Russian stocks or investments over there, and the only way to raise cash was to get out of securities that were doing well and had some liquidity. The situation is very similar to 1994 when the same thing happened."

Regardless of this situation, Michaelcheck believes that by employing hedging strategies and looking at risk-adjusted returns, he will be able to provide very good returns with very little risk.

"We do not move our money around," he says. "One of the

good things about our position is that we have a steady stream of good ideas."

Michaelcheck got the idea of offering a fund of funds when a number of people he called up asked him what he was doing with his own money.

"I was interested in taking a somewhat more aggressive amount of risk with some of my personal money, so I started a fund of funds for that, and then slowly people heard about it and asked if they could get in," he says. "I do not market it. It is basically people saying, 'What are you doing with your money?' and one thing leads to another."

This fund had approximately $60 million when we met, in which Michaelcheck was the largest partner. He was finding it easy to raise money, but difficult to find places to put it.

"There is a lot out there and it is hard to choose good places to put the money," he said, adding, "nineteen ninety-eight has been a bad year performance-wise all around and that is making a hard decision much harder."

When he invests money on behalf of the insurance company, he uses a model similar to Buffett's, but instead of picking stocks he picks hedge funds.

"We pick the hedge funds and allocate the money to various managers to invest for us," he explains. "The idea is to be moderately aggressive and invest in uncorrelated funds so that we are always able to capture some returns no matter what happens in the market."

Although he believes that he is correct generally regarding the ability to pick stocks, he does not believe this judgment to be absolute, so he has some of the insurance company's money invested in stock funds.

"I could be wrong and realize that, so I have put some money into some stock funds to cover myself," he says. "My gut tells me that people cannot pick stocks and those that do are just lucky."

Besides the structure of his organization, also setting Michaelcheck apart from other hedge fund managers is that the firm does not always go for the jugular when it moves in and out of the market.

"Our trading strategy is not very glamorous: Our philosophy is to stay rich and not get richer," he says. "We like to sleep at night and enjoy other obligations. When we get nervous, we realize that we are not doing what we set out to do and quickly get back on track."

NANCY HAVENS-HASTY

Clearly Wall Street is a place where the old boys' network is very much alive and kicking. No matter how far along things have come, it is still very hard for women to achieve the same prominence as men. Many women try and, for the sole reason of their gender, fail.

One woman who has managed to succeed is Nancy Havens-Hasty.

The fifty-something hedge fund manager, who has an MBA from Harvard and an undergraduate degree from Cornell, broke through the Wall Street boys' club in a very big way. Besides being the first woman elected to the Bear, Stearns & Co. Inc. board of directors, she is also considered by some to be the first woman investment banker ever to hit the Street. Now she is one of a handful of successful women hedge fund managers.

In 1995, she left the comfort of the Bear, Stearns & Co. Inc.—one of Wall Street's powerhouse firms, where she managed over 100 people, had responsibility for a trading account in excess of half a billion dollars, and was one of the company's 15 highest-paid employees—to start a hedge fund.

Her fund, Havens Partners, which had just over $50 million under management in the fall of 1998, specializes in risk arbitrage and distressed debt. With a team of six, Havens-Hasty trades the debt and equity markets looking for unique opportunities that she can exploit for a profit. In 1997, the first full year of operation, the fund was up a little over 15 percent, and when we met the fund was flat for the year.

"I left Bear, Stearns because I had gotten to a very narrow part of the pyramid and I knew that as a female I would not get any higher," she says. "I had got to where I got because I made money and I never had a losing year while I worked at the firm. When I got on the board, I suddenly found myself in a situation where it did not matter if you made money and it became 100 percent political, and I like making money more than playing politics."

Havens-Hasty, who is married and the mother of two children, believes that it would have taken an enormous amount of work and probably a change in her personality to move higher at Bear, Stearns, and she was not willing to do it. So she decided to leave and set up her own fund.

"I don't get my jollies from playing politics. I get my jollies from making money, and I realized that I should get myself into a situation where I could be happy full time," she says. "I enjoyed working within my own department and performing the research to get the job done but I did not enjoy the political aspects of the job."

Now Havens-Hasty works for herself and her partners to make money. Although she still has to deal with political/office issues like who the health care coordinator or the network administrator is, it's all for her own benefit. One thing that has taken getting used to is that when there is an equipment problem she can't pick up the phone and see immediate results.

"When I was at Bear, if my machine went down or something stopped working, I could call the help desk and they knew because of my title and position that they had to help me right away," she says. "Now there is no one to call and when we finally do get in touch with something we are always at the bottom of the list. It takes a lot of getting used to, but over time I am sure it will be well worth it."

Her initial interest in risk arbitrage came after a stint as an equity analyst covering the computer industry.

"I was looking for something that would keep me interested," she says. "I had been an investment banker and covered stocks and got bored. Arbitrage was very interesting to me at the time and it has become something I love."

Today the fund specializes in risk arbitrage and distressed debt, but because of market conditions it has very minimal positions in distressed debt.

"For the past year, distressed debt has been a pretty untenable place to be; default rates have been at an all-time low, and there were a lot of people who raised a lot of money in the early 1990s when defaults were at an all-time high, and they were all chasing a tiny bit of merchandise—and the risk-reward was bad," she says. "I got out of distressed about a year ago because there was nothing to buy and people were going all over the place looking for deals."

While some of Havens-Hasty's contemporaries looked to Indonesia and Korea for distressed debt deals, she says her research did not prove the investments worthy of her fund's capital.

"You don't buy Korea or Indonesia at 275 over," she says. "I would never buy those debt instruments because they don't honor contracts and you run the risk of ending up with nothing."

She did trade Latin America debt, in particular Brady bonds, when things got bad over there to take advantage of market opportunities. Brady bonds, named after former U.S. Treasury Secretary Nicholas Brady, are dollar-denominated international bank loans that have been converted into long-term debt instruments. Brady bonds, which are issued in U.S. dollars and are backed by U.S. Treasury zero coupon bonds, are used primarily by South American countries.

"When I don't know a market very well but it has totally fallen on its side, I will go in and buy the highest-quality instrument I can find and take the first 20 points out and let someone else have the next 30," she says. "That is the game I like. I am truly a vulture and I like it very much."

Since she has not been able to find distressed deals, Havens-Hasty has spent the bulk of her time doing garden-variety risk arbitrage. Her definition of that is going long the acquired company and shorting the requisite amount of the acquirer if it is a stock-for-stock deal. If it is a cash deal, she buys at the spread and works to protect herself should the deal fall through.

"In this type of market, it is very important to have the highest-quality deals you can find," she says. "If I think there is an enormous amount of downside I will buy puts to give up part of my upside to protect my downside. If the downside looks like a cliff, you don't want to be looking over the cliff without anything to hold onto."

One deal that she bought puts to protect herself with was the Monsanto Co. purchase of Dekalb Genetics Corp. The stock was trading at $90 a share when we met, but it had come up from being in the $40s.

"Since it started to perform, its major competitor has gotten shellacked, so you don't really know what the downside is. There were multiple bidders looking at this company, but the climate has changed and we really don't know what could happen," she says. "In situations like this when I want a position, I am going to do my best to protect myself. In this market the whole name of the game is protecting yourself."

As the market goes south, the deal flow is sure to dry up and when it does, Havens-Hasty plans on getting back into distressed situations.

"There will be lots of opportunities once the market shakes out," she predicts. "A lot of the distressed guys have been hit pretty bad because they have held on to their positions and now the competition in distressed is a whole lot less than it used to be."

The distressed market really took a beating in the second half of 1998. In one situation, Havens-Hasty had a position that she sold in March at around $37.25 (the market had been around $38.75, with a point spread). When she looked the position up on the screen, the market ranged from 18 to 25.

"Nothing had gone wrong with this situation. The spread which used to be two points is now seven. The market is really tough," she says. "I guess no one wants to buy and no one wants to sell it."

To get information on deals, Havens-Hasty uses a combination of internal analysis and standard Wall Street research. Having worked closely with the Street for so long, she has established a network of sources of information.

"We like to get information from people who know things, not just people who are repeating things they have heard from someone they don't really know," she says. "Whenever it is possible, I like to get in touch with people who really know what is going on so that I can make the best decision. Whatever is the problem with the deal or the area most likely to cause concern, I will try to figure out who I know who might have some insight on it."

When she started out, Havens-Hasty found that she was too busy just getting the business going.

"It was amazing to me how hard it was to start this business and how many stupid details there are that need to be covered in order to get things up and running," she says.

"We were last on the list for things to get done for many of the companies we work with and that was a big change for me coming from Bear, where people knew that if I had a problem it needed to be fixed immediately and properly the first time," she says. "When you are not a member of the firm any longer, everyone else comes before you."

In the past year or so she has been able to break away from those tasks and do what she likes to do: research.

"I like doing the research and finding deals," she says. "It is important to understand what is going on in a particular situation in order make sure you get the most out of it."

She also likes sticking to what she knows and understands.

"In order to be a good arbitrageur, you have to like to analyze a lot. It is like a game," she says. "It is about understanding the personalities and why the deal makes sense from a business standpoint as well as understanding what snakes are in the road between here and consummation. It is really a lot of fun because you are always learning something new and on the cusp of new technology."

Although she is constantly learning about new industries and companies, she does not believe in changing her strategy just to put up performance numbers. She thinks that when things start moving against her the best thing to do is to get out and wait for the market to turn.

"We will not have a position in our portfolio which is greater than 6 percent of our assets under management," she says. "I am not interested in taking unnecessary risks just to put up strong numbers. It is better to sit things out and wait for situations you understand than to go looking for things that you really don't understand and hope work out."

Havens-Hasty sees the most important part of her business as understanding how to manage risk and how to hedge to protect capital.

"Many people don't have any idea how to hedge or manage risk and therefore get into trouble," she says. "In order to be successful, you need to understand the instruments and how they trade, because if you don't, one deal can wipe out your whole business—especially if you are leveraged 11 to 1."

The main focus for her fund is to show strong results so she can continue to build the business.

"I want to work things out so that I can show the results that I want to show," she says. "I don't want to be below 15 percent—although in 1998 we will not do that—but I think that it will be feasible to post strong numbers as long as we continue to do what we know how to do."

Havens-Hasty believed that the fourth quarter of 1998 was going to be very ugly and that there was so much uncertainty in the market that it was unclear which way things were going to go. Although the market did come back to its pre-crash level by the end of November, she still felt that volatility was prevailing in all sectors.

"The best thing for us to do is to be ready for any direction in which the market would go," she says. "I think that we are on the brink of a real disaster, one in which the world goes into a major recession and takes us with them. The market could swing 400 points in either direction and we need to make sure we are prepared when and if that happens."

The fund ended up with a strong fourth quarter finishing the year up over seven percent. Havens-Hasty said she was able to take advantage of what she called "a mediocre market" that allowed her to "load up" on lots of bargains and ride the wave as the market recovered.

In 1999 the fund was having a good year; it was up over 16 percent through the third quarter. "We will survive through the downturns. What I would like to do is actually make money in this market," she says. "In order to do that, I have altered our strategy to be even more market neutral than we have been in the past."

Steps that Havens-Hasty has taken to alter her strategy include doing a lot fewer risky deals and taking much smaller positions as well as employing more shorts through the use of puts.

"Although Alan Greenspan lowered rates and it seems that the whole world is beginning to place values on investments for the first time in a few months, I don't think things are hunky-dory yet," she says. "I am not very hopeful, and that is why I own puts and also why our position size and use of leverage has gotten smaller."

Havens-Hasty does not think of herself as an active investor but rather as a passive one. Although she specializes in risk arbitrage, her methods differ from those of Guy Wyser-Pratte, who is profiled earlier in this chapter.

For example, one of the big arbitrage situations in the past few years was the Pennzoil deal. Like Wyser-Pratte, Havens-Hasty traded the deal, but she got out at over $80 a share when the deal first broke and then shorted it at $69 when the deal started to unravel. Her mistake was that she covered her short too early.

"I covered at $60 a share and now it is trading at $37," she says. "Net-net Pennzoil has been good to me and I wish that it had been the only thing I had traded all year. I don't believe in make-your-own arbitrage. I much prefer to observe and analyze and sort of sit in the grass."

One of the rules she lives by is something that a good friend who is a hedge fund manager told her when she was starting the fund: "Never bet the business on one trade."

When we met, the fund had approximately 20 partners but over 20 percent of the money under management was her own. She is really putting her money where her mouth is.

STEVE COHEN

Outside Wall Street, nobody seems to know who Steve Cohen is. He is never quoted in the newspaper, he is never profiled in magazines, and he has never been interviewed on television.

Yet in the hedge fund world he is a giant. His group of funds, called SAC Capital, manages over $800 million and on any given day he and his traders execute orders to buy and sell over 15 million shares of stock. To put this number in perspective, the average daily volume of shares traded on the American Stock Exchange is 28 million.

Cohen is probably one of the best-known unknown hedge fund managers in the world. He started his business in 1992 after spending a number of years trading stocks and options at Gruntal & Co. Since then he has built a business that has never had a down year and has grown to be one of the hedge fund world's most sought-after investments. Although Cohen was trained by experience while working at Gruntal & Co., his formal trading education came at a very early age.

"I am a tape reader," he says. "I learned how to trade stocks by going into my local brokerage firm office when I was 13 and watching the tape. From there, I was able to determine what was going on, how things were trading, and most importantly how to see opportunities from numbers moving across the screen."

Today his fund organization consists of more than watching the tape. SAC Capital employs over 130 people, who range from traders and analysts to back-office support and clerical people. The fund, headquartered in Stamford, Connecticut, with an office in New York City, has put up very significant numbers since inception.

In its first year, SAC managed approximately $23 million and posted gains of 17.49 percent, and the fund has never looked back. It has continually trounced the averages' postings in every year of its existence. The fund has consistently put performance numbers in the double digits. The fund's best year to date was in 1993 when it managed approximately $63 million and posted a gain of over 50 percent. In 1998, the fund was up over 40 percent while it was up over 50 percent through the 3rd quarter of 1999. When it comes to performance Cohen and his traders are on the ball.

Cohen still believes that knowledge of situations and ideas is the key to success.

"This is an information business and the only way to be successful is to pay attention to what is going on and find situations that make sense," he says. "One of the reasons we do as well as we do is because we cover most of the sectors in the S&P and also have unique trading backgrounds.

"We do not get married to positions. If things are not working the way that we had hoped that they would, we get out," he continues. "We don't just sit there and let things happen; we are very active and always making trades according to what is going on in the market."

As SAC has increased its assets under management it has also been constantly evolving its trading strategies, styles, and techniques.

"The more capital you have to move around the less you can move around as quickly, so consequently you have to develop a system that has a model that allows you to hold on to stocks even if the reasons why you went into the stocks have changed or your time frame has changed," says Cohen. "It is not a question of liquidity, because the markets are fairly liquid and we are in a lot of the big names. But the reality is as we have gotten bigger we need to have more reasons as to why we own something."

Cohen says that prior to opening SAC, when he was trading significantly smaller amounts of capital, he was able to buy 50,000 shares of IBM simply because he thought the market was going up. He based his decision solely on the tape and what he saw on the screen.

"I would make the decision to buy on the simple fact that I thought it was going up and I liked the way it looked without any fundamental reason as to why I liked IBM," he says. "Now we might buy IBM for a number of reasons. It might be that the computer sector is strong or that the analysts have expectations that things are going well. We now use different catalysts to make decisions as to whether we want to own something or sell something."

Cohen believes that one of the factors that has made his job harder is the explosive growth in the number of individual investors trading stocks—in particular those trading on the Internet. He believes that for the most part many of the investors trading electronically are momentum investors: When they see something go up, they buy it but don't have any real understanding of what is going on or why a stock's price is moving.

"My guess is that it is almost like a casino," he says. "The moves in stocks are larger and quicker than ever before and it seems like there is a bandwagon effect. When something is moving everyone wants to get on."

This has caused Cohen to adapt his trading style and pay closer attention to the price movements.

"If there is a piece of news out that I am going to discount because I don't think it is a big deal, normally I would go in and short the stock. But now I have to wait a little bit because things could get really crazy because there are so many other people involved in the game now," he says. "It is really unbelievable and I am going to make a fortune off of it."

One way Cohen has used the changes in the game to his advantage is with a trade in USA Networks, Inc., and its then newly listed subsidiary, Ticketmaster Online–City Search, Inc. In the last days before the initial public offering (IPO) of Ticketmaster, USA Networks stock started moving up and Cohen decided to short the issue. His experience told him that in most cases when a parent spins out a subsidiary, the parent's price gets a big run-up and then when the IPO hits—boom!—the parent falls like a rock.

Although Cohen would not say at what price he went short or at what price he covered, prior to the IPO the stock traded as high as $32 a share and then fell to $28. His short position consisted of over half a million shares.

"This is an example of how the phenomena of individual investors and Internet jockeys are causing the prices to move dramatically," he says. "USA Networks was discounted 12 times and the price still went higher because there is a lot of nonsense in the market right now. If the rules of the game had not been changed, this stock would never have gotten to be higher than $31 or $32.

"Nothing stays the same in this business," he continues. "You have to constantly adapt and evolve and learn what the new game is and then play accordingly."

SAC divides its capital into styles and sector portfolios run by various traders and fund managers. These styles surround a core trading strategy that Cohen runs with eight traders. He believes that having traders trade in groups allows the funds to be more profitable.

"I want people to be less worried about individual P&Ls [profits and losses] and more tuned into how the group is performing on the whole," he says. "For instance, if a guy has a bad day and is down a million bucks, the next day he is going to come in and not want to play the game. However, if the group account is up two million, he is going to come in the next day and still be in the game and will be trading. Maybe he had a bad day and did not score any points but maybe he had a few assists. We are trying a group approach, which over time will allow us to continue to perform extremely well."

The fund had approximately 75 investors when we met, including both individuals and institutions. Unlike other funds that charge fees of 1 percent plus 20 percent of profits, SAC has various fees based on the strategy or style the investor chooses. In some cases the fund charges as much as 50 percent of the profits without a management fee while other styles and strategies charge the standard 1-plus-20.

Cohen believes fees are justified by performance. In the funds' worst year, they were up 25 percent. Their best two months of 1998 were September and October, exactly when Long-Term Capital and a number of other hedge funds were having problems. Cohen believes his funds have benefited from the carnage that laid waste to the industry.

"We benefit from volatility because we are opportunistic and when the markets get a little more volatile there are more opportunities to trade," he says.

While Cohen is constantly changing his trading strategies to adapt to market forces he is also changing the structure of his company.

"I can see running as many as 10 different funds in the next few years," he says. "We want to be able to offer different strategies to meet the various needs of investors. Some people may want risk arbitrage while others want to invest in a specific sector. We are essentially going to create an organization that caters to whoever is interested in investing with us. I would call us a group of hedge funds under a single hedge fund roof."

Cohen, who was graduated from the University of Pennsylvania in 1977, got started on Wall Street in 1978 in Gruntal & Co.'s option arbitrage department after a friend of his brother's best friend got him the job.

"We basically would buy stock and hedge it with puts and calls," he says. "Back then it was a license to print money—everything was out of whack and it was really easy."

After a while, Cohen decided that hedging did not always make sense; he began to start holding on to positions and became a directional trader. When he first started trading at Gruntal he never spoke with anyone or used research reports; he made all his decisions based on what he saw on the screen.

"In the old days you could actually watch the tape and see what was going on," he says. "Now the tape moves too fast and there are more factors involved in trading and price movements."

Today, he is covered by all the major brokerages and is swamped with research reports and analyst recommendations. Still, he very rarely speaks with analysts or brokers and instead relies on his staff to handle the calls and countless pages of information.

"What we need to do is differentiate who is good and who is not and how to discount the investment banking aspect of the information that they are providing to us," he says. "When you get to know analysts over time, as the relationship grows, they will tell you things that can help you make a good decision."

Cohen hires both seasoned and unseasoned Wall Streeters to work at SAC. Lately, he has been hiring fund managers who could not make it on their own but who seem to thrive in the right environment—his.

"There are a lot of guys who try to run their own fund but have a hard time growing the business into something meaningful and end up nowhere," he observes. "Many of them realize that they would be much better suited in an organization where a lot of the stuff that they normally have to do is already taken care of.

"We have a few guys in our shop who were okay on their own, really nothing great, but who have just exploded since they have started working with us," he continues. "My guess is that there will be a shake-out in the industry when guys are not making any money, and I bet we will see a lot of guys who want to work with us."

Cohen is not sure how big he wants his fund operation to grow.

"I don't want to get big and put myself under a lot of pressure, but I would like to get big if it was managed the right way," he says. "In order to do that we would bring in talent and set up new funds, which would allow me to mitigate the risk and concentrate on what I know how to do without having to worry about how others are going to affect my performance."

As Cohen evolves his operation he adapts to the changes that affect all of Wall Street. One of the things that has really changed since he started in the business is the reliance on technology.

"It used to be you came in in the morning and you left at 4:30 and then you come in the next morning and you trade again," he says. "Now because of all the information that is out there, it has really become a 24-hour-a-day job. This job keeps going and going and going."

He says he isn't sure whether the change is good or bad but that the standard answer is that the job has become more interesting. The downside, of course, is that traders now have to sit in front of a computer all day and trading hours never end.

"This can be an all-consuming job but it is fun. Every day there is something new," he says. "It is a game. It's like playing a sport every day."

Hedge Fund
Investing

W hen it comes down to it, there is no science to picking hedge funds. For however many investors there are in hedge funds, there are at least as many different reasons why they picked that particular fund.

This chapter explains how various investors and consultants choose which hedge funds to invest in. Just as there are many different investment strategies managers employ to post returns, there are equally diverse ways to choose a hedge fund in which to invest. Hopefully, by reading this chapter you will gain a better understanding of how people choose managers, what to look for in a manager, and what to avoid.

Some people believe hedge fund investors throw darts at a list, while others believe investors perform hours of due diligence to determine which funds offer the right strategies, objectives, and management. Nobody really knows how people make their decisions, but one thing is sure: As Peter Lynch, the famed Fidelity Investments mutual fund manager, says, "People spend more money picking out the color of their refrigerator then they do on picking stocks." Lynch was talking about individual investors who do not have the wherewithal to invest in hedge funds, but the statement applies to sophisticated and unsophisticated investors alike. It was echoed by a number of people I talked to, including investors.

One of the problems with investing in hedge funds is all the misinformation published by both insiders and outsiders.

"The press very rarely gets the story right," says one industry observer. "They lack the deeper understanding of what hedge funds are really all about. Another part of it is that hedge funds do not do a good job of communicating what they do to the press. The third reason is that editors would rather have juicer headlines than get the story right."

The problem seems to be that the press does not understand that there are many different types of hedge funds with various strategies and risk-return profiles. For the most part, the press writes about two or three different individuals and assumes that they represent everyone. The press seems to focus on master-of-the-universe activities and the whole concept of shadowy figures moving markets.

"Once people understand that not all hedge funds are Long-Term Capital or Soros, Robertson, and Steinhardt," says Ron Lake, a hedge fund consultant, "then they will be able to understand what unique and exciting opportunities exist and are available to investors."

This being the case, it is quite clear why people look to hedge fund consultants and investment advisers, as well why many people in hedge funds don't necessarily know why they are in a specific fund or group of funds. Of course, one aspect of the funds, as with all investments, is greed. And one thing that comes with greed is hot money.

"A lot of people who invest in funds are doing so with hot money," says Steve Cohen. "These are people who put money with fund PDQ because it was up X percent last year and they believe it will do it again. However, as soon as the year-end comes and the fund does not meet expectations, boom, they pull their money and look to the next guy who is having or has had a good run."

Cohen says he believes most of the investors do not know why they get into specific funds. He feels that some of those who are not chasing hot managers are investing to feed egos or to keep up with the Joneses.

"People do very strange things when they invest," he says. "For the most part there is no rhyme or reason to their actions; they do it just to do it."

Cohen's sentiments are echoed by many of the consultants and analysts who help people choose fund managers and strategies. These consultants are investment advisers who specialize in the hedge fund world and for a fee will provide the investor access to their knowledge of the industry and its managers. As there are all types of investors, there are all types of advisers. Some work in conjunction with brokerage firms and hedge funds, acting as marketing agents for specific managers, while others work solely on behalf of the client and are paid a fee for their advice. For the most part, those who offer hedge fund consultant services do so on the up-and-up. Because the industry is so small relative to the mainstream investment world, it is not very easy to operate unethically or improperly for long. Still, investors need to beware of those who promise services that will lead to returns that are too good to be true.

Some of the most active hedge fund consultants are quoted in the popular press and interviewed on CNBC quite frequently. They are seen as able to provide an unadulterated view of the industry and of specific managers.

AN INVESTMENT ADVISER

Ron Lake runs Lake Partners Inc. in Greenwich, Connecticut, an investment advisory firm that works with individuals, family offices, and institutions helping them with asset allocation, manager selection, and running their investment programs.[1] Lake is not like other hedge fund consultants because he does not market funds nor does he sell a database of information on the industry.

Because all the firm's clients differ quite a bit from one another,

Lake can follow no specific guidelines to determine how to best meet clients' investment needs or to help them with investment decisions.

"We are basically investment staff for hire," he says. "Someone may come to us and say 'I have a pile of money and I would like to know how to invest it,' while other clients may come to us and already have investments in place and ask us to help them with various aspects of their programs."

At the end of 1999, Lake was overseeing over $1.5 billion of assets. In some cases he has discretionary power and can pull the trigger on investments, while in other cases, the client pulls the trigger as he and his staff advise. The investor pays Lake's company a percentage of assets for his services.

Lake uses a number of different methods when deciding where to invest. The first step is always to determine what the money is for and what the client's investment objectives are.

"I think you have to approach hedge funds in the context of some broader investment game plan," he says. "Investors need to do this partly because it just makes sense and partly because there are so many different hedge funds with disparate risk profiles that you can use funds in many different ways either to augment returns or risk or to do both, depending on the investment program."

Lake believes that hedge fund investors are no different than other investors. Some are very clever and some are not; some stop to think about issues, while others do not.

"You need to understand the role you want hedge funds to play in your investment portfolio before you start talking about what kind of funds are appropriate," he says. "Once you establish what kinds of hedge funds are appropriate, you can then start talking about specific funds in which to invest."

According to Lake, some people hire his firm because they are looking to be educated, while others hire him because they want someone to bounce investment ideas off.

"There is no hard-and-fast rule or pattern to the motivation or behavior of the investor," he says. "This is partly because of the diversity of clients we work with, and also because some are very heavily involved in hedge funds and tend to be a more sophisticated investor and some are relatively new to it and tend to have a smaller allocation to it."

Once they determine the context for the investment (return objectives, liquidity, and risk tolerance are among other criteria), Lake determines what role hedge funds can play in the portfolio.

"If someone is a very conservative investor who has a lot of fixed-income assets with conventional equity investments, he or she might look to hedge funds as a way to get absolute returns from totally different areas," he says. "They may want a more aggressive piece, perhaps geared to macro managers—something totally different from anything else they are already investing in."

Lake says each client usually wants something different from his or her hedge fund investment. While the press may lump all hedge fund investors into a single category, he believes no two are alike.

"You may have two different types of investors who represent four different types of investment approaches based on what they want to accomplish," he says. "One can't build a house without building a foundation and as such we work very hard to understand the investment objectives in order to provide the right advice."

Lake's company typically plays a continuing role with clients, usually working with them for a number of years, establishing and building an investment program. Once investments are working the way clients want, Lake usually hands them the reins to handle on their own.

One of the big issues surrounding hedge fund investing is understanding what the potential conflicts of interest are between the investment adviser, broker, or third-party marketer and the fund manager.

"What bothers some people in the industry is when people wear two hats—one as a consultant, one as a marketer—and one is hidden under the other without full disclosure," he says. "With third-party marketers who are purely third-party marketers, things are simple—everyone knows that they are marketers—and consultants tend to be consultants; but there are a few that wear multiple hats. The problem only comes up when people don't make it clear where they are coming from."

Lake thinks that the hedge fund industry is really a bunch of different industries under one umbrella and that for the most part things are pretty stable in the hedge fund universe.

"The hedge fund industry is the same as the health care industry in that there are all kinds of people doing all kinds of things. At any one point in time, some parts are doing well while others are not—and sometimes at the expense of others," he says. "Right now there is a lot of concern among investors that certain hedge funds have failed to live up to their promise and are losing assets to withdrawals while other funds as a result are attracting more capital."

In the wake of the carnage of 1998, the press was quick to report that turmoil had taken over the industry and that investors were withdrawing capital from funds en masse. Lake believes that most of the press got the story wrong.

"The press talked about how there are all these redemptions and all this turmoil but they missed the rest of story," he says. "The rest of the story is, yes, there were redemptions, but some of that money was being recycled to other funds and for the most part the capital was staying with alternative investments."

Lake believes that one of the biggest problems with understanding the hedge fund world is the lack of knowledge about its diversity.

"Some people seem to have a hard time understanding that there are hedge funds with all different styles and strategies and, like mutual funds, some will do well and others will not," he says. "Our job is to provide the customers with the right information to allow them to make an informed decision based on their investment needs."

AN INSTITUTIONAL INVESTOR

For the most part, when one reads or hears about hedge fund investors, people think of rich individuals and wealthy families. While these groups are very active in investing in hedge funds, institutional investors are by far the largest and most important user of such vehicles.

These pension funds, insurance companies, banks, brokerages, and national and multinational corporations represent hundreds of billions of dollars invested in everything from plain-vanilla stocks and bonds to exotic derivatives and hedge funds.

Most of the investors operate in strict secrecy. An unwritten rule forbids these investors and the funds to disclose who does and does not invest with specific funds.

"You will never get a fund to give up the name of an institutional investor because they represent too big an amount of investment dollars," says an industry observer.

To understand the process that institutional investors use to determine where and how much they will invest, one needs to get to the investment decision maker.

Unfortunately, most if not all institutional investors hesitate to explain their allocation and investment strategies on the record. One institutional investor who is very active in hedge funds agreed to be interviewed, but only if no names were used.

The pension fund is charged with managing $20 billion. At the end of 1998, it had allocated 8 percent of its assets to hedge funds. It plans to increase the allocation to possibly more than 12 percent by the end of 1999. When we spoke in December, it was invested in five hedge funds, all of which manage their money internally and use long/short market-neutral strategies. It plans in 1999 to add hedge funds that invest more aggressively.

The institution's philosophy is to pursue investments at the forefront of the pension investment process to be able to make additional returns. It is willing to do things that other pension funds are not.

"If the others are not making the investment for a pure risk issue," says one of the pension fund's managing directors, "and if we think that is one of the primary reasons for not making the investment, we believe it will create extra returns for our portfolio."

The pension fund tries to control risk very tightly where its managers believe risk can become an issue. So, for example, it exercises very tight controls over its fixed-income program and moderate controls over its U.S. equity program.

"Exercising control allows us more latitude to take more risk with a long/short program or a higher-returning market-neutral and absolute-return strategies," explains one of the pension fund's managing directors.

"We have chosen the funds we are with because we believe that fundamentally they have unique insight and investment capacity and capability coupled with excellent risk controls," the managing director says. "Those three attributes are consistent throughout our entire investment program and we believe by applying them to hedge funds—which turns the dial up a little bit—we will be able to attain significant returns without adding significant risk."

The institution believes that investing in long/short strategies provides for a more efficient use of its capital. As such it plans on moving money from long-only managers who focus on matching the indexes to long/short managers who focus on individual stock selection.

"By changing our strategies we believe we are going to be able to leverage our managers' ability to add value and hopefully increase returns at the same time," the managing director says.

The pension fund allocates money by looking at the track record and diversification the hedge fund managers bring to the program. If they pass the review, the fund allocates between $100 million and $500 million to them.

"We will add managers as we add assets," the managing director says. "But we also realize that managers have a life span and some of our managers are decaying, so the trick for us is to determine when a manager has reached the top and then move on to another fund. Hopefully, we can get out of the fund before it hits bottom. The real test to the program is to not hold on to one fund too long."

The pension fund plans to drop three of its hedge funds, managing $2 billion, in the next year and plans to add five additional hedge funds to its portfolio.

The pension fund limits its stake in a particular fund to 20 percent of its total assets. It believes that the best way to add value to its portfolio is to find young managers and grow with them.

"We are a big fund and it does not make sense for us to screw around with a $10 million dollar chunk," the managing director says. "We are looking for a manager that can grow into becoming a $2 billion fund, and if this is the case we may start with a $50 million position and grow with the fund to the point of allocating it $200 million to $300 million."

The pension fund doesn't use consultants to help pick hedge funds but its executives believe that as it expands, they may do so. They plan, for example, to hire a fund of funds manager to gain access to some hedge funds that it otherwise would not be able to invest in.

"When it comes to investing in hedge funds, people are very conscious and cognizant of making sure *due diligence* is performed and the right choices are made," the managing director says. "We want to be very thorough and dig under the surface of the funds to make sure that we do not make a mistake and as such we realize that we cannot do it on our own.

due diligence   questions by investors to the manager regarding investment style and strategy as well as the manager's background and track record.

"The advantage of hiring a fund of funds manager is that you can get into some funds where there is a smaller slice available—say a $10 million or $15 million piece," he continues. "Also, we can insulate ourselves from the risk perspective and we can blame them if things do not go well."

The pension fund will look for fund of funds managers the same way it looks for individual fund or money managers. It will choose a fund of funds that has a competitive edge, can be trusted, employs good risk control, and can share due diligence as well bring good funds to its portfolio.

"It is not simply a risk-versus-return issue with a fund of funds," the managing director says. "We are looking for a partner that can help us expand our use of hedge funds."

The managing director believes that many institutional investors make investment decisions based on historical attributes and the manager's reputation rather than looking ahead at how the manager could be expected to perform. While he believes this is a mistake for anyone, it can be a disaster with long/short hedge funds because it is a leveraged bet.

"There is a lot more risk associated with long/short investing than many believe," he says. "And you have a lot more riding on the manager's skill than with someone running a large-cap growth fund, so you have to be a lot more careful about picking this type of fund manager.

"I don't think many institutional investors are taking the extra level of thoughtfulness that is required with these types of investments," he continues. "Although one can never be sure what is going on in someone else's organization from appearances, this seems to be the case."

One of the nice things about having so much money is the pension fund's ability to be aggressive about pushing down fees, asking a lot of questions, and being really nosy about how the fund is being managed.

"Some people do not want to do business with us because they think we're too involved in the operation," the managing director says.

Some hedge fund managers' egos do not allow for pushy investors. One hedge fund in particular has not been willing to negotiate its fees because it believes it can replace the pension fund's dollars with someone else's in a heartbeat—and at a higher fee.

"We have not pulled the money out of this fund because we are greedy and we want the returns," the managing director says. "Just because they don't want us does not mean we do not want them. This is totally a game of egos and if we can put our ego aside then we are going to make more money than another plan sponsor who cannot put their ego aside."

The pension fund speaks with its hedge fund managers on a monthly or bimonthly basis and it reviews the funds' performances and positions daily. If a questionable situation arises, the pension fund managers are quick to call to find out what is going on.

"We are always sort of checking ourselves, saying this is what the market is doing, this is what we expect from a manager, and this manager is not acting in sync with the thought, so we need to understand why," the managing director says.

The pension fund's managers believe that now is the time to expand its exposure to hedge funds.

"There has been a lot of learning going on in the industry with other people's money and many investors have been scared away, and the opportunity is right to expand our program," the managing director says. "It is up to us to go in and pick people that we think will be the best going forward."

THIRD-PARTY MARKETERS

To be successful, hedge fund managers need only strong performance numbers and capital. Most people in the hedge fund world subscribe to the *Field of Dreams* theory: "If you build it, they will come" when it comes to raising money. If the fund performs well, investors will come. Still, building a track record takes a lot of work, and managing a hedge fund does not always provide for time for raising capital.

"It is one of the hardest parts of the job," says one fund manager. "When I started my fund, I knew I could pick stocks and put up good numbers but I had no idea how to raise money, nor was it a skill I was interested in learning."

As the hedge fund industry has grown so has the business of raising money for funds. Gone are the days of fund managers relying solely on family and friends for the bulk of the assets they manage. Sure, most funds start out that way, but once things get going, managers need to look outside their circle to the world of wealthy individuals, family offices, and institutional investors. To reach these people, many fund managers team up with third-party marketers. These firms specialize in raising money for funds. For the most part, they receive a fee for the assets they raise as well as a trailing fee for however long that capital and any new capital that their clients invest remains with the fund.

The world of potential investors is in reality much larger than it seems. As the stock market rallies, options are granted, companies are bought, and the economy stays strong, many more people and institutions become wealthy enough to meet the Securities and Exchange Commission's requirements needed to invest in hedge funds. Even with the carnage of 1998, hedge funds remain hot, especially those that performed well for the year. Still, a hedge fund manager needs help in getting his or her story out, someone who has the databases and, more important, the relationships with investors.

One person who does is Conrad Weymann. His firm, called Mallory Capital Group, is located in Darien, Connecticut, and works with fund managers to raise capital from institutional investors. To operate as a third-party marketer, Weymann, who has a Series 7 license, is associated with a National Association of Securities Dealers member firm, and has a very large database of pension funds, endowments, foundations, commercial and investment banks, and family offices. All have one thing in common: They are looking to make investments that will provide them with significant returns.

"Once we find a manager we like with a good record or story, we try to get them to engage us to raise money for them and then go at it," he says. "We basically make a lot of phone calls, sound out lots of information, and set up meetings with the intention of getting the clients to invest with the manager."

Weymann started in the industry six years ago after a friend persuaded him that he would be good at it. He had previously worked at Comdisco, a technology company, setting up private equipment leasing deals with Fortune 2000 companies and the institutions that bought the deals for the tax credits. The first job for his new career came from a large hedge fund consulting firm that wanted to set up a fund of funds for institutions structured in master trusts.

"When we started to work on this project in 1993, hedge funds were all the rage and had a lot of appeal," he says. "The institutions were very interested in what we were doing because the idea of a fund of hedge funds allowed us to spread the risk and balance over all sorts of strategies."

Unfortunately, as the Fed tightened interest rates, the economic landscape changed dramatically and the project never got off the ground.

"What initially seemed like a very good idea very quickly became something the institutions did not want to take to their boards," he says. "But it got me involved in the hedge fund side. As an investor with Julian Robertson, I had some familiarity with the business and thought that raising money for the hedge funds looked like a good opportunity."

Weymann says that he believes that the carnage of 1998 is going to make his job a lot harder.

"There were a lot of expectations that when the markets corrected hedge funds would have protected their investors, but that has been proven wrong," he says. "Many institutions that were moving toward hedge funds with those thoughts in mind have decided to look elsewhere. To some extent, the industry has let the investors down."

He believes that the real winners of 1998 are funds that have a good track record and that demonstrate time and time again that they can put up solid returns.

"The good guys who, say, are good at stock picking, have some flexibility, are not too large, use some leverage, and have the freedom to make some moves will be able to continually outperform the market and be able raise capital," he says. "Those investors that did experience some disappointment in 1998 will probably shift to a different manager, but investors are not going to give up on hedge funds."

Weymann typically tries to work with one fund at a time. Why? He does not want to cross swords and contact an investor twice, and he wants to make sure he gets paid for his work.

"It really does not make sense to work any other way," he says. "If we did we would end up wasting a lot of time and effort and not be able to make a living."

Weymann typically gets a percentage of both the manager's management fee and performance fee. If he brings in $10 million and the manager charges a 1 percent management fee, he will earn $10,000 from the management fee as well as a percentage of the performance fee at the end of the year. The length of the fee arrangement ranges from one year to forever and is usually scaled down from the first year. For example, he may earn 20 percent of the performance fee in the first year, 10 percent for the next five years, and 5 percent for the final years.

"The fee structure really varies from manager to manager because no two situations are alike," he says.

Weymann finds institutional investors through directories and databases. In some cases, he knows the people he is calling on, while in other situations he is calling on prospects cold. The idea is to learn about the investors' ideas for investments and come up with situations that match the ideas.

"It is easy to get lists of institutions that have alternative investment programs," he says. "It is harder to find high-net-worth individuals and family offices, and you really have to rely on people helping with introductions and references. One guy tells you about another guy and so on and slowly you are able to build up a book of business."

AN INDIVIDUAL INVESTOR

While institutions invest enormous amounts of money in hedge funds and represent the bulk of dollars in the industry today, individual investors also play a significant role. Most of the large funds tend to have a mix of institutional and individual money, while many of the smaller funds, those under $300 million in assets, usually consist solely of high-net-worth investors and family offices.

"When you start out, the first people you go to are friends and family and friends of your friends and family," says one hedge fund manager. "It is hard to attract an institutional audience and it is even harder to get them to invest in a new fund or even a relatively new fund with somewhat of a track record."

One manager told me that the bulk of the money that he used to launch his fund came from clients he had as a stockbroker at Lehman Brothers. "These people knew me, trusted me, and believed in my ability to pick stocks and make money," he says.

One individual who invests in hedge funds through a small family office is a doctor in Newport Beach, California. The doctor, who requested that his name not be published, told me his father had decided a number of years ago that the best way for the family to maintain its wealth would be to pool its resources into a family office.

"The family office allows us to take advantage of our belief in the efficient market theory," he says. "We believe that you need to look to alternative investments as potentially yielding a better rate of return with potentially the same if not lesser risk ratios."

The family office invests in a core group of funds that meet the needs of most of the family, while allowing individuals to invest in other funds, too. The idea is to make sure that everyone is provided for and that those who can tolerate risk do so and those who cannot do not. The doctor's mother, for example, who is 82, is in a core fund that all the family members invest in but she is also in a fixed-income fund with no one else in the family. Four nuclear families take part in the family office, with a total of nine individuals.

"This has not been without missteps. Just like stocks or mutual funds, sometimes the managers we choose do not work out," the doctor says.

One of those missteps was with one of the family office's core funds. The fund, which specialized in capturing profits from earnings surprises, did not turn out as well as planned and therefore the family had decided to the leave the fund in early 1999. The doctor planned to replace the fund with a well-known New York equity arbitrage fund.

"I felt that they were not putting up the numbers they should have been and decided that it would be better to look elsewhere for returns," he says.

The remaining core group of investments consists of two funds. One specializes in mid-cap stocks while the other invests in the oil services sector. "Our mid-cap managers are not young guys that have not been around the block, and they invest very similarly to Warren Buffett. The fund consistently provides us with steady returns year after year. It is really a great fund for us," he says.

The doctor found the mid-cap stock managers after he decided that it was time to leave a private bank and look elsewhere for returns. "I basically ran spreadsheets on domestic equity managers and found that the fund was better than anybody else in performing in up and down markets," he says. "We found the other fund through a person we use as a sounding board for ideas who recommended it to us."

The oil services fund has proved to be very successful. Although the fund was down approximately 15 percent in 1998, it had been up 60 percent in 1997 and 90 percent in 1996. "We use the oil services fund because we believe in the industry and it provides us with a hedge for the overall market," he says. "It has performed well for us and even though it is down this year, it is not down as much as the rest of sector, so we know the manager is doing something right."

The doctor, who also acts as the managing partner without pay, does most of the research to find fund managers. He reads everything he can get his hands on and speaks to brokers, advisers, and investors around the country. "Finding hedge fund managers is sort of a net-working kind of thing," he says. "I found one manager when I read about him in a *Barron's* article. I called him to schmooze with him and we have become friends."

The doctor also fields calls from third-party marketers and brokers who are paid to raise money for funds. The doctor says it does not bother him when these people call because they often provide him with information. "You have to evaluate everything for yourself and you surely cannot take their word for it, but there is really no harm in talking to them," he says. "These people don't make money from my end of the transaction."

The doctor does all his own due diligence and he recommends funds to the family, but each member makes his or her own decision. For example, his sister has chosen not to go into the new core fund. Instead she is looking for an investment that will provide her with a steady stream of cash rather than superior returns year after year.

As the managing partner, he evaluates everything from track records and previous employment to *Sharpe ratios*, risk-reward ratios, and *standard deviations*. He is self-taught and learned almost everything he knows about finance from eight feet of financial books he keeps in his home. In some cases, he works with a few consultants and pays them a fee for investment advice.

"I keep extensive files and information on funds that we invest in currently and on those funds that we may invest with in the future," he says. "On average I probably spend less than four hours a week on following the funds. I spend more time worrying about individual stocks that I trade on my own than on how the funds are performing."

Sharpe ratio the ratio of return above the minimum acceptable return divided by the standard deviation. It provides information of the return per unit of dispersion risk.

The doctor and his wife have invested in a fund that specializes in distressed securities, while the other family members have decided against it. "We chose to invest in a distressed fund because we believe it is a wiser thing to do than individual investments, because sometimes these things go belly-up," he says. "By being in the fund we are able to have 15 positions instead of three or four and are protected against the downturns."

standard deviation a measure of the dispersion of a group of numerical values from the mean. It is calculated by taking the differences between each number in the group and the arithmetic average, squaring them to give the variance, summing them, and taking the square root.

The doctor runs the family office on a laptop computer that he uses to administer what he calls portfolios. These portfolios are either limited liability corporations or limited partnerships. Each of the portfolios, of which the family office has three, provides the members of the family access to specific funds.

"No one has ever gotten upset because an investment wasn't

successful," he says. "What they do get upset about is when I don't get them performance figures as quickly as they think they should be made available."

For the most part, the doctor tends to stay away from the marquee names in the hedge fund world, instead looking for funds that he can grow with along with the manager.

"It is a small family office that allows us to invest tax efficiently and to find managers with good tax-efficient returns, in turn protecting and maintaining our wealth, " he says. "We are not doing it for tax avoidance; we are doing it to make superior returns over time."

A CONSULTING FIRM

When people ask what is the best investment bank on Wall Street, the answer is always Goldman Sachs Group. It is the premier investment house in the world and, whether or not people admit it, other houses want to be like it.

When it comes to hedge fund consultants the situation is very similar. One firm stands above the rest in terms of prestige and power: Boston-based Cambridge Associates. The firm, which was started in 1975, specializes in providing endowments and nonprofit organizations with investment and financial research and consulting and advisory services.

Cambridge Associates prides itself on being totally independent and a firm that works solely in the interest of its clients. It does not earn fees from financial institutions or money managers nor does it manage money.

"We are consultants in the true sense. We do not manage any money; we do not have a fund of funds; we strictly give investment advice and keep it objective," says a spokesperson. "We have no economic incentive to recommend one product over another."

The firm would not comment on its clients but they are believed to include 48 of the 50 biggest college endowments and many large foundations. One expert says the firm probably has over 700 clients investing in 500-plus hedge funds. The investments range from $1 million to $50 million and for the most part are spread between five and 10 funds.

Cambridge Associates does not market to colleges, but it does provide services through the use of sophisticated databases to help colleges see what their peers are up to.

"We give our clients investment advice and help them with asset allocation and manager selection," the spokesperson says. "Our biggest value-added is our research of alternative investments, both the nonmarketable side of the investment world, which are private equity and real estate, and the marketable alternative, which is hedge funds."

The firm keeps a list of hedge funds it likes and meets with about 10 hedge fund managers a week in its search of good investment vehicles. It gets between 30 and 40 calls a day from hedge funds looking to crack the institutional market.

"Any hedge fund that calls one of our clients is usually referred to us, and if we do nothing else, we act as a screen," says the spokesperson.

The first thing managers are told to do when they call is to send in material that details what the fund does and how it does it. Cambridge Associates picks through the stack of candidates and looks for funds that seem interesting. If, upon further review, the hedge fund is deemed interesting, the manager is invited to the office for an interview. About one in 10 of funds that call in is invited; one in 10 of those invited turns out to be a keeper.

"When they come in they give their presentation and we put them on film; we have them all on video," says the spokesperson. "If we like what we see, we really go deep. We will go visit them at least two or three times, we will get current and historical portfolios, and then we start digging from there."

The firm checks references, does Securities and Exchange Commission checks, and leaves no stone unturned before it recommends a hedge fund to one of its clients. "We look at whether a fund makes sense for a specific client on an isolated basis," the spokesperson says. "Usually the client provides us with a long list of criteria that the potential fund has to meet before we can recommend it to them.

"The universe of hedge funds ranges from unleveraged convertible arbitrage funds all the way up to the global macro players and every variation in between," the spokesperson adds. "So we are trying to make sure [the fund we recommend] fits with the clients' investment objectives and does what they are trying to do."

Cambridge Associates has found that many managers are willing to show them more than they show most other people because foundations and endowments are such fertile ground. The industry is inclined to believe that the money from these institutions stays longer than investments from offshore entities and funds of funds, which tend to move out faster. The theory is that institutional money may be harder to raise, but once it is in, it is in for good.

"We like to be early and if a manager has good background, a good resume, and, more important, a good strategy, we will look at them," the spokesperson says. "The key to a good strategy is to be in an inefficient area of the market because we do not pay for brilliance. Paying 1 and 20 percent to buy GE does not make a lot of sense, so we are trying to look for some inefficient area of the market were the manager can make some sense and can add value, long and short. It always boils down to if the guy is worth the fee, because most guys are not worth 1 and 20. It is a huge haircut for an investor to take."

Clients go to Cambridge Associates to receive advice on their entire investment program. The firm usually does everything from acting as a referee with the investment committee to making sure they keep the portfolio conflict free to developing and adding structure to the investment program.

"A lot of clients come to us who have 30 managers, ranging from cash managers to fixed-income hedge funds, equity hedge funds, and private equity funds and they look to us to add structure," says the spokesperson. "We probably got a hundred new clients last year; half of them had hedge funds and probably half of them did not know why they had hedge funds. We try to figure out what bets they are making because these things are called 'absolute return' or 'market neutral' vehicles and there really is no such thing."

Cambridge Associates believes 99 percent of hedge funds make directional market bets or what it calls in-directional bets. For example, some funds bet on liquidity and execute convergence trades, which are long something that is illiquid and short something that has liquidity. The fund is billed as one that can outperform its peers, regardless of market conditions, but when times like August 1998 come along and only liquidity counts, these types of trades blow up.

"In each case, we are trying to distill the strategy into what bets they are making and where the value-added comes from," the spokesperson says.

Cambridge Associates has some clients that have been investing in hedge funds since the days of A. W. Jones & Co. and Michael Steinhardt's first fund. Some of them are very sophisticated and have board members who run their own hedge funds or who have managed money professionally, while others have no money management experience.

"Sometimes the boards use us as a sounding board or they may come to us with an idea and we go run it down for them," says the spokesperson. "It really varies from client to client as to what they want from us and what we do for them."

The firm has also started building a client base with family offices, in particular those with over $1 billion in assets. Many of those clients need a lot of hand-holding and they come to the firm to get basic and completely original investment advice.

Cambridge Associates is paid either by the hour or as a percentage of assets. It does not earn any commission from fund managers.

"We have no discretion over any of the money," he spokesperson says, "so in the end all our clients come to us for the same thing: investment advice that they know is conflict free and completely objective."

A MANAGER OF MANAGERS

Although the rest of us eventually grow up and out of it, in the hedge fund world some people still like to hold their MOM's hand: that is, the hand of their manager of managers.

A manager of managers acts as an adviser to investors who are looking for a money manager but do not want to deal with the day-to-day responsibilities of managing those investments and do not want to go into individual hedge funds or a fund of funds.

A MOM will customize multimanager alternative investment strategies for institutional and high-net-worth investors. The strategies include the use of hedge funds, managed futures trades, and foreign exchange trades. Although MOMs have their fingers on the pulse of the markets, they do not try to time the markets. One of the benefits of using a MOM is that doing so provides the investors with both freedom and control over their investments—two characteristics that are rare in today's alternative investment world.

These organizations exert enormous amounts of control over the managers they invest with. The MOM usually requires the manager to sign a contract that details exactly what the manager can do with the money and provides for next-day redemption if the manager violates the contract. These organizations pick and choose individual money managers for their clients. The managers operate separate accounts for each investor. In most cases, an investor creates a portfolio of managers to handle all alternative investment needs.

One such MOM is a company called Parker Global Strategies LLC. Started by Virginia Parker in 1995, it currently has 14 employees in its headquarters in Stamford, Connecticut, two employees in Japan, and over $500 million under management.

"What makes us different from a fund of funds is that we are in control of what is going on with the money and the manager at all times," she says. "We tailor the contract with the manager according to what we are ready to do with the client's money. This means that we are always going to hire managers to run their strategy the way they typically run it. We don't want to ask them to do something they normally don't do or do something that may inversely impact their performance."

The contract that Parker signs with managers is very thorough. Not only does the contract describe the trading strategy in detail but it also includes limits on leverage, value-at-risk limits, and which instruments the manager is allowed to trade, as well as a list of those the manager is allowed to use as a counterparty. "If, for example, options are an integral part of someone's strategy, then they may be eligible to one manager but not to another manager with whom we allocate," she says.

Not all managers are willing to succumb to the controls Parker and other MOMs place on them. Those who do seem to make it all worthwhile. "There are more than enough very, very good managers out there, which means that we can provide some real value-added to our clients," she says. "The reason managers have been willing to do this is that they respect the work we are trying to do for our clients and look at us as a source of capital that provides them access to many different sources of funds through one entity."

Once a manager is chosen, Parker's company monitors trading activity daily. The firm independently marks to market every trade daily, unless it is something fairly illiquid, in which case the position is marked to market weekly. Parker also runs the positions through a risk monitoring system and monitors the activity to ensure that it is following the trading policy specified in the contract.

In some cases, the MOM knows more about the manager's portfolio than the manager does. For example, a manager who does not use value-at-risk or stress testing analysis may be able to learn something from Parker.

"It is not unusual on the risk side for our firm to know more than the manager on a quantitative basis," she says. "If managers do not know this information, it does not mean they are not good traders. All it means is that they probably did not work in a banking environment, at least not when those tools were becoming standard practices."

Parker likes to know what is going on with the manager. Although the firm is always looking for new managers, it primarily sticks with a core group of traders. Once she finds a manager she likes, she visits and asks the manager to complete a very detailed questionnaire. If Parker likes what she reads, the firm sends in a team of people to perform operational and risk management due diligence. The team looks at the manager's accounting practices, systems, and models, and checks references.

"Then we try to negotiate a contract with the manager," she says.

At the end of 1998, the firm was using 22 managers, with allocations of $5 million to $22 million with each. It is not unusual for Parker and her staff to speak with the firm's clients and managers every day.

"We have a very high degree of comfort with most of our managers," she says. "Our philosophy is that once we find a good manager that still has capacity, we want to be the ones to use that capacity rather than just go try to find more and more managers."

In almost every instance Parker has the traders manage money for her clients in a separate account, but it has gone into a third-party fund a couple of times. Then the manager must meet specific requirements, including 100 percent transparency and next-day redemption capability.

Parker says that because of the amount of information and control she requires, there needs to be a lot of trust and a lot of both sides wanting to work together. "This is a relationship business, and we like to focus on relationships that are working well," she says.

In late 1998, Parker was managing $500 million, a large portion of which was with managers. The firm did maintain a significant cash position to fund a guaranteed structure that it manages. For the most part, Parker's clients are banks and the customers of banks. The company manages the banks' own capital, while for their customers it creates private-label products that are marketed directly to institutions and corporations. The firm is paid both a management fee and a performance fee.

Parker also operates the first publicly registered and largest hedge fund in Japan. Marketed as a closed-end fund through IBJ Securities, it was started in March 1998 and requires a minimum investment of $1,000. Its shares do not trade in a public market.

When it comes to picking managers to work with, Parker likes to rely on word of mouth and her experience. She talks to people who allocate large sums of money, asking them whom they know, whom they see, and most important whom they like.

"I have never been able to find a manager in a database," she says.

"In my experience having a database is the least important element in finding good managers."

Parker uses a network of large banks and insurance companies as well as people who have been in the industry for years to get information and ideas on managers. "There is a lot of camaraderie in the industry, and I think that a lot of people have a vested interest in giving each other tips on who is hot and who is not and try to help keep people out of trouble," she says. "There is a lot of very good information that is shared that is not readily available."

If Parker finds that a manager is not complying with the contract, she can end the relationship. Although it has never happened (most managers fix problems when they are told they are not in compliance), it is an aspect of the business that makes it unique in the alternative investment world.

The return clients receive ranges from 10 percent to 30 percent, depending on the strategy that is being used. In late 1998, Parker used traders that employed strategies ranging from global macro and convertible arbitrage to U.S. and European stock long/short and managed futures.

Her company has stayed away from a number of strategies because of their risk, Parker says, explaining why the firm uses managers employing high-yield, emerging markets, and mortgage strategies.

"We do have a couple of managers that we like in high-yield and we were ready to allocate and decided not to this summer because of what was happening in the market," she says. "We are not quite ready to allocate to these strategies but do plan on going to them in the future."

Parker believes that being a manager of managers offers much more control than being a fund of funds operator. She says that she knows of a lot of smart fund of funds managers who found that a number of their managers were going to markets outside their normal routine and they wanted to redeem. These managers put in their redemption notices and by the time they could redeem the assets were gone—all lost.

"When you operate a fund of funds, you have no control," she says. "Even to be a fund of funds manager with 100 percent transparency, you don't have control if you can't get out, so what good does it do you?

"Our way allows us access to invest possibly with the same managers, but we are able to do it on our terms," she continues. "At the moment there are plenty of good managers that are willing to take money on our terms and therefore we have a business model that we like a lot."

Typically, Parker and her staff try to follow the market and get an understanding of what is going on, not in an effort to time the market but in an effort to stay out of trouble.

"Our views on the markets can cause us to have some small shifts in allocations but typically not huge, dramatic swings," she says. "Ultimately, the allocations are my call, but the principals here work together, talk, and share views, and usually we come up with a consensus on which we base our decision."

Parker believes that in light of the carnage of 1998, people now more than ever understand the value of risk management.

"In August, September, and October we were up because of the way we do things," she says. "It was because we had the control, which meant that we had the capability not to be allocating in some places and very quickly shift allocations to a few managers who had good performance during those periods. Our control really made a huge difference."

Conclusion

Hedge funds have become a topic du jour as a result of the carnage of the summer of 1998. It was an exciting time to be following the industry. For the first time in the five years I have been covering hedge funds, there was a real buzz about the industry beyond Wall Street's inner circles. Every day the phone would ring with stories of this fund losing money or that fund going out of business, while this fund had performed well and these people were getting set to raise some more capital. As Virginia Parker said of her business, the hedge fund world has a lot of camaraderie. Nobody ever wants to hear of a fund manager going out of business or someone who sustained enormous losses, even if they are vying for the same investors and in some cases the same investments. The industry is closely knit, from the accountants and lawyers to the prime brokers and the traders to the fund managers and the investors. The hedge fund world is a small part of Wall Street that has many, many more years of success ahead of it.

Unfortunately, the usual story about hedge funds shows something else: wealthy people investing with a secretive fund manager to earn enormous amounts of money and living lavishly and happily ever after. Every now and then there is a story about excesses like the helicopter to work or the 50 cars coupled with the huge shopping sprees. There are very few positive stories written about the hedge fund industry. There are even fewer to which the average person can relate. Instead the stories play on jealousy while exposing greed and making most people long for the wealth and privileged life that hedge fund investors and managers seem to have.

Well, here is a story with an entirely different spin:

On December 23, 1998, I got a message on my answering machine from Paul Wong, the Midas trader who runs Edgehill Capital in

Old Greenwich, Connecticut. The message said, "Dan, call me—I have an interesting story to tell you." I figured that the story had to do with Long-Term Capital. Earlier in the day, the story broke that Meriwether and his partners stood to make a small fortune from their performance in the fourth quarter. I figured Wong was going to give me some color on the situation. I was completely wrong. When Wong and I finally spoke on December 24, he told me one of the greatest stories about hedge funds that I have ever heard.

About five years ago, Wong got a call from the brother of a boyhood friend. The gentleman called Wong in desperation. It seemed that he had been doing some math and realized that the money he had been saving for his daughter's college education would be nowhere near what he needed. His brother suggested that he call Wong and ask for help. When the two spoke, Wong told the gentleman about the hedge fund he was starting and that he thought it would make sense for him to put his daughter's education money to work there. The father agreed, figuring that if Wong was putting his own money in the fund, it was as good a place as any for his money. He invested $45,000 as one of Edgehill's first investors. He had good years, like 1995 (up 134 percent) and 1996 (up 24 percent), and a bad year in 1997 (down 7 percent). Edgehill was up over 41 percent in 1998, and through the first six months of 1999 the fund was up 10 percent.

Throughout it all, the gentleman stayed with Wong. Toward the end of December 1998, Wong got a call from the father, explaining that he would need the money the following fall to pay his daughter's tuition at the University of New Hampshire. Although he was not surprised because he had been following the performance all along, he was quite happy. On December 24, 1998, his $45,000 had grown to over $125,000, enough to pay his daughter's college tuition and then some.

"Everyone thinks that hedge funds are about greed," says Wong. "In reality, hedge funds are about providing people with capital to do things that are important to them. What better reason to go to work every day than to know that the money you make is going to provide for a child's education?"

This story is not unique. There are many cases where fund managers and investors have used the proceeds of their investments to do great things. Two of the world's greatest philanthropists are George Soros and Michael Steinhardt, who combined give tens of millions of dollars away each year to help those less fortunate. Alfred Winslow Jones, the father of the industry, did not live a lavish life, but instead gave a lot of his money away, helping to make New York a better place to live. The list of hedge fund managers and investors who do good things with their wealth goes on and on.

Hedge funds do not destroy markets or ruin the economies of countries. They are simply private investment vehicles that seek significant returns regardless of market conditions. Managers are paid handsomely when they make those returns. It is a win-win situation for both investors and managers.

The problem comes when the managers step out-of-bounds and make mistakes. Then it is for the investor and the manager to determine how best to solve the problem. The idea of government influence, intervention, and regulation is not wise. It can only hurt the industry and its investors. The more government involvement, the worse things will be. Members of Congress, senators, and government regulators who have very little knowledge of money and markets should stay away from regulating the industry.

In a capitalist society, we subscribe to the theory that markets correct themselves when errors occur. If the market deems hedge funds too risky or too expensive or no longer valid investment choices, then the market will force a change. Until that day comes, the government and securities industry regulators need to keep out of the business and let the chips fall where they may. If they do not, there may be a lot more parents who cannot afford to send their children to college and a lot fewer men and women philanthropists.

Appendix

Hedge Funds Strategies

The following is a list that defines a number of hedge fund styles and strategies. The information was compiled by Nashville, Tennessee–based Van Hedge Fund Advisors International, Inc.*

Aggressive Growth: Expected acceleration in growth of earnings per share. Often current earnings growth is high. Generally high P/E, low/no dividends. Usually small-cap or micro-cap stocks which are expected to experience very rapid growth.

Distressed Securities: Buying the equity or debt of companies that are in or are facing bankruptcy. Investor buys company securities at a low price and hopes that company will come out of bankruptcy and securities will appreciate.

Emerging Markets: Investing in the equity or debt of emerging markets. These countries tend to have high inflation and high, volatile growth. The definition of an emerging market is the market in any country with per capita GNP (gross national product) of U.S. $7,620 or less in 1990 (World Bank).

Financial Services: Manager invests at least 50 percent of portfolio in the securities of banks, thrifts, credit unions, savings and loans, insurance companies, and/or other financial institutions. Currently available quarterly only.

Fund of Funds: Manager invests in other money managers or pooled vehicles that may utilize a variety of investing styles, creating a diverse investment vehicle for investors. The manager may or may not choose to reveal to investors the funds in which he or she is invested.

Healthcare: Manager invests at least 50 percent of portfolio in the securities of healthcare products; pharmaceutical, biomedical, and medical services, and/or other healthcare companies. Currently available quarterly only.

Income: Investment with a focus on yield/current income rather than solely on capital gains and appreciation over time.

Macro: A global or international manager who employs an opportunistic, top-down approach, following major changes in global economies and hoping to realize profits from significant shifts in global interest rates, important changes in countries' economic policies, and so on.

Market Neutral—Arbitrage: Manager focuses on obtaining returns with low or no correlation to the market. Manager buys different securities of the same issuer (e.g., the common stock and convertibles) and works the spread between them. For example, within the same company the manager buys one form of security that he or she believes is undervalued and sells short another security of the same company.

Market Neutral—Securities Hedging: Manager is long some securities and short others, with no real correlation between long and short plays. Presumably, net exposure to the market is reduced because if the market moves dramatically in one direction, longs might lose but shorts will gain and negate the move, and vice versa. If longs selected are undervalued and shorts overvalued, there should be net benefit.

Market Timing: Large commitments to one or two asset classes depending on economic or market outlook. Frequently, a portfolio will be invested 100 percent in either stocks, bonds, or cash equivalents. Anticipates/predicts timing of when to be in and out of markets.

Media/Communications: Manager invests at least 50 percent of portfolio in the securities of companies involved in telecommunications, the media, publishing, information technology, the manufacture of cellular products, and/or other information services. Currently available quarterly only.

Opportunistic: Manager changes from strategy to strategy as manager deems appropriate. Can utilize one or many investing styles at a given time and is not restricted to any particular investment approach or asset class.

Several Strategies: Manager employs various specific, predetermined strategies in an effort to diversify approach, for example, using "Value," "Aggressive Growth," and "Special Situations" strategies in tandem to realize short- and long-term gains.

Short Selling: Strategy is based on finding overvalued companies and *selling* the shares of those companies. The investor does not own these shares, but is anticipating that the share price of the company will fall and borrows the shares from his or her broker. Ideally, when the share price does fall, the investor buys shares at the new, lower price and thus can replace, to the broker, the shares sold earlier, thus netting a gain. This strategy is also employed where the investor believes share price will fall due to company problems, and so on.

Special Situations: Usually event-driven. Manager takes significant position in limited number of companies where situations are unusual in a possible variety of ways and offer profit opportunities: for example, depressed stock, an event in the offing, offering significant potential market interest (e.g., company is being merged with or acquired by another company), reorganizations, or bad news emerging which will temporarily depress stock (thus manager shorts stock).

Technology: Manager invests at least 50 percent of portfolio in the securities of electronics companies, hardware and software producers, semiconductor manufacturers, computer service companies, biotechnology, and/or other companies dealing in high technology. Currently available quarterly only.

Value: Manager invests in stocks that are perceived to be selling at a discount to their intrinsic or potential worth, (i.e., undervalued) or in stocks that are out of favor with the market and are "under-followed" by analysts. Manager believes that the share price of these stocks will increase as value of company is recognized by the market.

Glossary

accredited investor   an investor who meets the Securities and Exchange Commission guidelines required for investing in hedge funds.

arbitrage   a financial transaction involving simultaneous purchase in one market and sale in a different market.

bear market   prolonged period of falling prices.

bull market   prolonged period of rising prices.

derivatives   securities that take their values from another security.

draw down   percentage of loss during a given period.

due diligence   questions by investors to the manager regarding investment style and strategy as well as the manager's background and track record.

fund of funds   an investment vehicle that invests in other hedge funds.

leverage   means of enhancing return or value without increasing investment. Buying securities on margin is an example of leverage.

limited partnership   a legal term used to describe the structure of most hedge funds and private investment vehicles.

long position   a transaction to purchase shares of a stock resulting in a net positive position.

management fee   fee paid to the manager for day-to-day operation of the hedge fund.

margin call   demand that an investor deposit enough money or securities to bring a margin account up to the minimum maintenance requirements.

offshore fund   an investment vehicle that is set up outside of the United States and is managed from a low tax jurisdiction that is not available to U.S. citizens.

onshore fund   an investment vehicle that is set up in the United States that is available to U.S. citizens.

performance fee   fee paid to manager based on how well the investment strategy performs.

poison pill   any number of legal defensive tactics written into a corporate charter to fend off the advances of an unwanted suitor.

portfolio diversification theory   the theory assumes that investors want the least possible dispersion of returns for a given level of gain.

prime broker   service offered by major brokerage firms providing clearance, settlement, and custody functions for hedge funds.

quantitative analysis   security analysis that uses objective statistical information to determine when to buy and sell securities.

Sharpe ratio   the ratio of return above the minimum acceptable return divided by the standard deviation. It provides information of the return per unit of dispersion risk.

short position   a transaction to sell shares of stock that the investor does not own.

standard deviation   a measure of the dispersion of a group of numerical values from the mean. It is calculated by taking the differences between each number in the group and the arithmetic average, squaring them to give the variance, summing them, and taking the square root.

volatility   the degree of fluctuation over a given period in a security based on the standard deviation of the price.

Endnotes

Chapter 1 Hedge Fund Basics

1. *The Wall Street Journal* Staff, "Tiger Fund Has September Loss of $2.1 Billion," *The Wall Street Journal*, September 17, 1998, page C1.

2. These numbers were verified with Tiger Management's spokesman Fraser Seitel of Emerald Partners Communications Counselors on December 15, 1998.

3. The profit would be slightly less because there is some cost associated with the use of leverage.

4. Diana B. Henriques, "Fault Lines of Risk Appear As Market Hero Stumbles," *The New York Times*, September 27, 1998, pages 1 and 28.

5. This is the only firm to earn money on its investment. Many firms made a lot of money trading with Long-Term Capital as its broker.

6. Diana B. Henriques, "Fault Lines of Risk Appear As Market Hero Stumbles," *The New York Times*, September 27, 1998, pages 1 and 28.

7. Wyndham Robertson, "Hedge-Fund Miseries," *Fortune*, May 1971, page 269.

8. Ibid.

9. An accredited investor is defined by the Securities and Exchange Commission as an individual or couple that has earned $200,000 or $300,000 respectively in the past two years and will do so in the next year, or has a net worth of a million dollars. A super-accredited investor is a person and/or a family that has net investable assets in excess of $5 million.

10. Bethany McLean, "Everybody's Going Hedge Funds," *Fortune*, June 8, 1998, pages 177–184.

11. Ibid.

12. Reprinted from the March 1949 issue of *Fortune* by special permission; copyright 1949, Time Inc.

13. John Thackray, "Whatever Happened to the Hedge Funds?" *Institutional Investor*, May 1977, pages 70–73.

14. Carol J. Loomis, "Hard Times Come to the Hedge Funds," *Fortune*, January 1970, pages 100–103, 134–138.

Chapter 2   How Hedge Funds Operate

1. Carol J. Loomis, "Hard Times Come to Hedge Funds," *Fortune*, January 1970, pages 100–103, 134–138.

2. *The Wall Street Journal*, February 2, 1998.

3. Neither the Soros organization nor Mr. Niederhoffer would comment as to whether the funding came from the Soros organization. It is pure market and industry speculation.

4. Elsa Chambers, editor, and Sarah T. Fullilove, assistant editor, "1998 Prime Brokerage Survey," *Global Custodian*, Spring 1998.

5. It is the norm in the industry that the broker/marketer who brings investment dollars to the fund gets a piece of the fees that the dollars add to the fund's bottom line.

6. This comment is for illustration purposes only. It is not to imply that either fund manager farms money out to other managers.

7. James M. Clash, "Wretched Excess," *Forbes*, April 20, 1998, pages 478–480.

8. Michael Siconolfi, "Bond Market Still Punishes Hedge Fund and Investors," *The Wall Street Journal*, October 5, 1998, page C1.

9. KPMG Peat Marwick, LLP/RR Capital Management Corp., "The Coming Evolution of the Hedge Fund Industry: A Case for Growth and Restructuring," March 1998.

10. Carol J. Loomis, "Hard Times Come to the Hedge Funds," *Fortune*, January 1970, pages 100–103, 134–138.

11. Ibid.

12. Stephanie Strom, "Top Manager to Close Shop on Hedge Funds," *The New York Times*, October 12, 1995, page D1.

13. Ibid.

14. I must make it clear that these numbers are used for illustration purposes only. It is impossible to confirm exactly how much money the Soros organization—or any other hedge fund for that matter—earns and receives for its efforts.

15. Most money managers meet and visit executives at companies they either are planning to invest in or already own.

16. *The Wall Street Journal* Staff, "Business Week Agrees to Settle Libel Suit Brought by Investor," *The Wall Street Journal*, December 18, 1997, page B6.

17. "A Hitchhiker's Guide to Hedge Funds," *Economist*, June 13, 1998, page 76.

18. Bob Davis, "Rubin Says Speculators Didn't Cause Asia Crisis," *The Wall Street Journal*, July 1, 1998, page A2.

19. International Monetary Fund Occasional Paper 166: "Hedge Funds and Financial Market Dynamics," May 1998.

20. Ibid.

21. Ibid.

Chapter 4 Hedge Fund Investing

1. Lake Partners Inc. also acts as a consultant to a fund of funds company called the Optima Group, helping with manager selection, monitoring managers, and structuring investment programs. At the time we spoke, Lake was not a marketing agent for Optima Group.

Index

203